HEROES
of
WORLD WAR II

HEROES
of
WORLD WAR II

Tom Bower

FOREWORD BY
General Sir Peter de la Billière

BCA

LONDON   NEW YORK   SYDNEY   TORONTO

For Alexander

First published in Great Britain in 1995 by
Boxtree Ltd, Broadwall House, 21 Broadwall, London, SE1 9PL

This edition published 1995 by BCA by arrangement with Boxtree Ltd.

Text © Bookmoat Ltd 1995
Foreword © General Sir Peter de la Billière 1995

1 3 5 7 9 10 8 6 4 2

CN 4522

Designed by Robert Updegraff
Picture research by Anne-Marie Ehrlich
Origination by Adelphi Graphics
Printed and bound in Frome Somerset by Butler and Tanner

A CIP catalogue entry for this book is available from the British Library

Foreword

"I am very conscious that for every one I mention there are a hundred others whose doings were just as worthy of record."

So said the World War II commander for whom I have the greatest respect – Field Marshal The Viscount Slim. Slim is my hero. Modest, courageous in battle, and possessing moral courage of the highest order: a great leader of men and a man with the resilience to survive defeat in Burma and turn it into victory.

War, by its nature, offers opportunities for courage and the making of heroes that seldom present themselves to the person in the street. At the same time outstanding courage in battle, where risking life and limb is part of one's duty, is bravery of the very highest order. In most cases it is accompanied by an outstanding example of leadership unrelated to rank or position.

Those recognised with gallantry awards are deeply conscious of the selectivity of their award: they hold the other members of their unit with a special regard. Whenever I have written to congratulate an NCO or officer on his gallantry award it is almost without exception that in their reply they tell me it is a team award and the honour is shared with their mates.

In war, to recognise one man's bravery is to acknowledge the professionalism and the courage of his whole unit. A unit with several of its members decorated will feel pride; each person will feel his own small contribution is recognised and he will himself feel spurred on to greater achievement. He too will feel a bit of a hero.

I have the privilege of knowing a few of the World War II holders of the Victoria Cross. Stanley Hollis of Normandy fame took my Staff College syndicate over the ground where he won his award. Away from the exploding shells, the threat of anti-personnel mines, the stammering of the German machine guns, he is a quiet, likeable Englishman: the man with whom to enjoy a pint in the local. Dick Annand won his Victoria Cross with the Durham Light Infantry. 'Oblivious of mortars and machine gun fire he repeatedly dispersed the Germans with grenades which he carried in a sandbag. Thrice he personally repulsed the Germans – he just went mad.' Yet Dick Annand, with life-long suffering from his war wounds, is a delightful gentleman: modest, kind and lacking in any apparent aggressiveness in his make-up. Yet when the moment demanded it these two men stood out from their fellow soldiers by displaying unique courage and having no regard for their own lives: they became public heroes.

Courage is an expendable quality and each of us has his own level of credit. A man with a small level of courage may well push himself to greater extremes than someone with a greater credit level. He may not distinguish himself so much in the eyes of others but he will have sacrificed more and suffered greater demands than his more outwardly courageous companion. This is why I have always respected the courage of 'the hundred others' without whom no commander or leader can fight his ship, his aircraft or his army division effectively.

My greatest personal hero is my father. He died saving others as his ship sank in the Battle of Crete. He gained no medal: he did nothing extraordinary – along with others he did his duty – he gave his life for his shipmates, his friends, and his country. But to one small boy he became an instant hero and remains one for me to this day: he has inspired me throughout my life.

Each one of us is a hero to someone – we may not know to whom but we have inspired them and we hold a responsibility to them. This book tells us of some of our nation's most famous heroes from World War II: they would wish you to remember 'the hundred others'.

General Sir Peter de la Billière, KCB, KBE, DSO, MC, MSc, DL

Introduction

For those children like myself growing up in the ruins of post-war London, the memories of playing on bomb sites, ration coupons for food and the vision of limbless men shuffling in the streets, remain a searing impression.

Our childhood games in the school playground were invariably of soldiers at war. The most fortunate boys were those possessing bits of uniform, steel helmets and even a live bullet passed on by fathers and uncles. So, not surprisingly, my earliest sympathies were for the heroes who had sacrificed their lives in World War II. I have always counted myself as one of the fortunate beneficiaries.

On my weekly trips to the local library as a boy, I went directly to the shelves stacked with books about the war. Accounts of escapes from POW camps, the pilots of the Battle of Britain, the tribulations of SOE agents in occupied France and especially the daring of the commandos fed my appetite for accounts of the heroism by those committed to ridding the world of evil.

There were few war films which I did not see at least twice. Even now, I recall emerging in tears from the cinema after seeing the Cockleshell Heroes, hating the Nazis for executing those brave, ordinary Englishmen.

I have another vivid childhood memory of Germany. During my first visit in 1950, I was staying overnight with my parents in a half-demolished hotel in the ruins of Cologne. Lying in my bedroom on that first night, I heard German men in the tavern downstairs singing in loud voices the Nazi marching songs which had been their rallying chorus just five years earlier. White-faced, my mother explained that Germany's military defeat had not expunged the Nazi philosophy. Twenty-five years later, I began my hunt for Nazi war criminals and exposed in my first book, *Blind Eye to Murder*, how the Allies had deliberately failed to prosecute the German organizers and executors of the worst crimes in Europe's history.

Other books and television documentaries followed, showing how Nazi scientists, doctors and soldiers had been secretly recruited by British and American officers despite their horrendous crimes. Throughout those years of solitary work, I always thought of the British servicemen and women – the heroes of World War II – who had died fighting for a just cause, unaware that their ultimate sacrifice would be cynically betrayed by those who had never risked their lives in combat. Whenever I demanded from often self-satisfied British politicians, civil servants and others who recruited or protected the Nazi war criminals an explanation for that betrayal, I was greeted with a shrug. To say the least, their self-justification was distasteful.

With this book I have completed the circle. Those heroes mentioned in this book are naturally just representatives of the tens of thousands who suffered and died. In reading the full accounts of their deeds, I experienced again the shivers and even tears as in childhood – imagining the excitement, the horrors, their courage and their pain. Thanks to them, my generation and those that followed were given the opportunity to enjoy free, decent lives. It is not only Britons but all Europeans who owe their thanks to our heroes. For Britain's heroes also died to allow not only young Germans and Italians the chance to grow up in fine, democratic nations, but also the youth of Eire, Switzerland and Spain, neutrals during the conflict, to enjoy the benefits without the cost.

To all those who served, we salute their courage and sacrifice. To the heroes, we give special thanks, because by their example they set the standards not only for Britain in wartime, but also in peace. For whenever we are appalled by an act of moral cowardice or criminal dishonesty, one thinks, albeit subconsciously, back to the heroes' ultimate sacrifice. Whatever the tribulations and inadequacies of modern Britain, the irrefutable truth remains that at Europe's darkest hour, there were vast numbers of Britons prepared to wage the just war and the continent's peace and prosperity owes much to their sacrifice.

In writing this book, I owe particular thanks to Eric Taylor for his historical research, to Anne-Marie Ehrlich for her splendid achievement in producing the memorable photographs and to Robert Updegraff for assembling text and photographs with his arresting design. It is dedicated to Alexander, my youngest son aged 4, who already appreciates the qualities of leadership and courage!

TOM BOWER
MARCH 1995

Narvik – Norway

9 April 1940

Seven months of phoney war was abruptly broken on 9 April 1940 in the Norwegian Sea. On HMS *Glowworm*, Lieutenant-Commander Gerard Roope *(left)*, 40, from Somerset, spotted the *Admiral Hipper*, a German cruiser seven times bigger than his British destroyer.

Britain's pride was still the Royal Navy, unchallenged, commanding the world's biggest fleet of warships, patrolling the waters to protect the Island Kingdom. Spontaneously, the senior service challenged the aggressor in an inevitably one-sided duel.

HMS *Glowworm's* end was brutally swift but instead of abandoning his battered and burning warship, Roope rammed *Admiral Hipper* and fired one more salvo, damaging his foe. Roope's brave defiance and sacrifice (he went down with his ship) was rewarded by the Victoria Cross – the first to be awarded in the war.

By then, the Royal Navy's supremacy was being blown asunder by Hitler's unexpected, audacious and successful invasion of Norway.

Through a snow storm raging the following day, Captain Bernard Warburton-Lee *(right)*, 45, from Wales, led five destroyers to Narvik. His mission was to prevent German occupation of Norway's ice-free port.

The German U-boats and destroyers guarding Narvik were taken by surprise. Warburton-Lee opened fire, sinking and damaging three destroyers and six merchant ships. 'When our torpedo hit we saw a flash,' reported a British crewman, 'and it was just as if some huge hand had torn the German ship in half.'

Suddenly, from a neighbouring fjord, five unseen German destroyers emerged, their guns blazing at the British intruders, sinking or damaging four of the Royal Navy attackers. Among the wounded was Warburton-Lee, hit on the bridge. He died being towed through the water to the shore.

Warburton-Lee's sacrifice was not in vain. Another British task force soon arrived to sink eight more German destroyers and a U-boat. In the euphoria Warburton-Lee was awarded the Victoria Cross.

But the Royal Navy's glow quickly dimmed. During the evacuation of British troops from Narvik on 7 June, two destroyers and HMS *Glorious*, an aircraft carrier, were sunk by the *Scharnhorst*. 1,500 men died.

The Invasion of France

Unexpectedly, out of the clear dawn over France on 10 May 1940, the Luftwaffe struck with a vengeance and destroyed nearly 400 British and French airplanes. As the blitzkrieg pushed ferociously towards Paris, 1,600,000 British and French soldiers, stirred from eight months of phoney war. In northern France, the British Expeditionary Force rushed forward to stop German panzers speeding into Belgium and Holland.

Awestruck and terrified by the German vehicles and troops crushing through their country, Belgian resistance was sporadic and often non-existent. When the 'impregnable' Belgian fortress of Eben was captured by German parachutists, the RAF was urgently summoned to bomb a key bridge across the Albert Canal to stop the panzers' advance.

Leading the attack by five woefully outdated Fairey Battle bombers, Flying Officer Donald Garland, 22, from County Wicklow (*left*), flew through intense anti-aircraft fire to drop his bombs. Unfortunately the raid was unsuccessful: only one plane returned to Britain, and Garland was killed. Yet his bravery was recognised by a Victoria Cross.

Like all the other dead heroes, the old melody resonated for the sacrifice:

When you go home,
Tell them of us and say
For their tomorrow,
We gave our today . . .

Churchill

1940

'Winston is back' was the message of relief flashed around the Royal Navy when Churchill, the former First Lord of the Admiralty, returned to Government at the outbreak of war.

Born in Blenheim Palace in 1874, Churchill's unique understanding and unrivalled experience of warfare, politics and history infused the British with spirit and vitality at their darkest moment.

Instinctive, perceptive, energetic, critical and encouraging, Churchill's appointment as Prime Minister on 10 May 1940 sparked a revolution in Britain's approach to the war.

The British bulldog, pointing 'V' for Victory, standing on the beaches defying the loathsome Nazis, rallied Britons to fight, suffer and even die for their country's supreme value: democracy and the defeat of tyranny.

With a German invasion imminent and the nation's defences limited, Churchill's oratory was magical: 'I have nothing to offer but blood, toil, tears and sweat . . . we shall defend our island, whatever the cost may be, we shall fight on the beaches, we shall fight on the landing grounds, we shall fight in the fields and in the streets, we shall fight in the hills; we shall never surrender.'

And if Britain was conquered, urged Churchill, let men still recall in one thousand years: 'This was their finest hour.'

Retreat from France

By 11 May 1940, the British Expeditionary Force had neatly fallen into Hitler's trap by moving forwards into Belgium. Four days later, outmatched and demoralised, the British were retreating towards Arras, France, the Army's operational headquarters.

Simultaneously, in the south, Hitler's generals had delivered their surprise hammer blow. Pushing through the Ardennes forest into France, the panzers, the Luftwaffe and the Wehrmacht had crushed French resistance and swung north, slicing through French lines, threatening to cut the British off.

Around Arras, on 21 May, British tanks staged one magnificent counter-attack against a German tank division. Among those valiantly fighting was Company Sergeant-Major George Gristock, 35, The Royal Norfolk Regiment. Ignoring the natural instinct to take cover and survive, Gristock, leading eight riflemen, moved forward to block the enemy's breakthrough. Shot in both legs, he crept to a safe position and killed four Germans manning a machine-gun. Evacuated to Britain, Gristock died of his wounds and was awarded the Victoria Cross.

By 24 May, brave, desperate and ultimately forlorn, the remnants of the British tank force was in retreat.

Lieutenant Christopher Furness, 34, Welsh Guards (*left*), was ordered to cover the withdrawal. Leading an attack with light tanks, Furness fought until all his vehicles had been destroyed and then led his men in hand-to-hand combat. In that bitter struggle which cost many German lives Furness was killed.

His death, rewarded by the Victoria Cross, was not in vain. Stunned by the British counter-attack, General Erwin Rommel, the German commander, temporarily halted his advance, so granting valuable time for the British retreat to Dunkirk.

Dunkirk

26 May to 3 June 1940

The heroism of Captain Harold Andrews (*inset*) on the outskirts of Dunkirk during the night of 31 May 1940 fuelled the politically necessary myth of the 'Dunkirk spirit'.

'Operation Dynamo', the evacuation of 338,000 British, French and Allied troops on about 900 ships, succeeded thanks to a fierce rearguard action stalling the German armies.

Unlike the many who waited lamely on the nearby beaches to flee, Andrews positioned volunteers from a company of the East Lancashire Regiment in a barn near the Canal de Bergues. At dawn, as German soldiers crossed the waterway, Andrews and his men killed at least 17 enemy and only withdrew as their wooden defences splintered and burst into flame.

Every minute counted as the armada of 'little ships' – masterminded by Admiral Sir Bertram Ramsay, a trusted and respected sailor recalled from retirement – crossed the Channel under the withering fire of the Luftwaffe and German E-boats and brought the remnants of the British Expeditionary Force back home to fight another day. Among those rescued was Lieutenant Richard Annand who, wounded and faint after killing many Germans with hand grenades, risked his life to rescue his batman.

The fighting spirit of Andrews and Annand at that moment of defeat made eventual victory possible. Both were awarded the Victoria Cross. 'Wars are not won by evacuations,' Churchill told Parliament, 'but there was a victory inside this deliverance.'

The Luftwaffe attacks Britain

4 July 1940

The sense of isolation of Britons in July 1940 combusted into anger and defiance against brazen Nazi air attacks.

Some like Able Leading Seaman Jack Mantle, 20, (*above*), from Wandsworth, London, were especially courageous. On 4 July, during a Luftwaffe air raid on Portland, Mantle continued firing a 20mm pom-

pom gun from the starboard of HMS *Foylebank* even after a bomb had shattered his leg and other wounds were sapping his life. He died at his gun post, shooting to his bitter end. Undoubtedly, his Victoria Cross was awarded to inspire others to commit themselves to sacrifices in the future when the battle hardened.

Air Vice-Marshal Keith Park

Masterminding the Battle of Britain at No. 11 Group, Fighter Command in South-East England was Air Vice-Marshal Keith Park, 48 (*right*), a quiet, devout New Zealander who joined the Royal Flying Corps as a fighter pilot.

Park's skill was his control at all levels of the men and *matériel* needed to fight the ceaseless battle. His organisation co-ordinated not only the pilots and the planes, but also the ground crews, headquarters staff and most importantly, radar and radio-listening officers tracking the Luftwaffe and analysing their conversations.

Working well with Chief-Marshal Sir Hugh 'Stuffy' Dowding, the father of Fighter Command, Park insisted that it was more important to shoot down German bombers than to challenge the Luftwaffe's fighters.

The statistics proved his victory. Between 15 August and 15 September, Fighter Command lost 493 aircraft and 201 aircrew killed; the Luftwaffe lost 862 aircraft and 1,132 air crew killed. On 15 September Hitler recognised he had not won air supremacy over Britain and postponed the seaborne invasion, 'Operation Sealion'.

The Battle of Britain

In August 1940 – a flaming crest in the Battle of Britain – the RAF's 644 fighters were pitted against 2,600 Luftwaffe planes.

The pilots – 'The Few' – were a gung-ho band of brave young men, eagerly awaiting the Tannoy call: 'Scramble. Bandits!' Running across the grass towards their Spitfires and Hurricanes to speed off the runways, none could ever be sure they would survive to enjoy that night's singsong and pint at the bar. Outnumbered but supreme in spirit, these men were Britain's sole defence against Hitler's 'knock-out blow', the first step for the invasion of Britain.

Among those pilots was Flight Lieutenant Eric Nicolson, 23 (*left*), 249 Squadron, from Hampstead, London. On 16 August, the day the Luftwaffe flew over 1,700 sorties, Nicolson, flying a Hurricane, was hit. Wounded in the eye and foot and his plane ablaze, Nicolson was on the verge of baling out when he spotted a Messerschmitt in his gun-sight. Lunging back into his seat, he pressed the blistering gun button. Screaming, 'I'll teach you some manners, you Hun,' he pursued the zig-zagging enemy at 400 m.p.h. into the sea.

As the dashboard melted, Nicolson lurched out of the cockpit, somersaulted in the air and pulled the ripcord, parachuting to safety. 'All I'm anxious about now is to get back flying and have another crack at the Germans,' he told the *Daily Telegraph*, nursing an extra shot wound from a Home Guard sergeant who mistook him for a German pilot.

Nicolson won the only Victoria Cross of the Battle, but it was shared by all, blessed by Churchill's famous words of gratitude: 'Never in the field of human conflict was so much owed by so many to so few.'

Reginald Mitchell

Designer of the Spitfire

'This is it, chaps,' gritted Wing Commander Brendan 'Paddy' Finucane (*left*), Fighter Command's 21-year-old ace as smoke trailed from his Spitfire over the Channel.

Flying too low to bale out, Finucane crash-landed into the sea. There were seconds to clamber out, but Finucane, probably knocked unconscious, sank with his Spitfire leaving an oily patch on the sea's surface.

No pilot blamed the Spitfire, which was the outstanding fighter of the war, outclassing the Messerschmitt, thanks to its designer Reginald Mitchell (*far left*) and Rolls Royce's new Merlin engine.

Born near Stoke-on-Trent in 1895, Mitchell was fascinated from childhood by airplanes. After an apprenticeship, at 24 he was appointed Chief Designer at Supermarine Aviation Works.

In three successive years Mitchell's seaplanes won the world speed record. By then he was overcoming the obduracy and technical shortsightedness of civil servants in the Air Ministry to design a new fighter aircraft. The specifications were precise – fast, high rate of climb, good all-round visibility for the pilot, easy to maintain, designed for mass production and well armed. It was first test flown in 1936. Mitchell spelled out his approach to the design: 'Good technical know-how without common sense usually resulted only in mediocrity.' The Spitfire's debut was spectacular. 20,000 would be built during the war but Mitchell did not witness his success. In 1937, he suddenly died aged 42.

Throughout the war, as pilots reported deficiencies, captured German fighters revealed unknown advantages and Rolls Royce improved the engines, Mitchell's successors constantly improved the Spitfire – often without the Air Ministry's sanction.

The Blitz – Britain's 'finest hour'

Captain Michael Blaney, 30 (*below*), from Essex was among that core of dedicated Royal Engineers summoned to undertake the patient, precise and perilous task of defusing unexploded bombs littering London and other cities during the Blitz.

The threat of German bombers causing havoc had preoccupied British governments before the war. Plans for civil defence had been laid, but the ferocity of Hitler's terror campaign beginning in August 1940 had not been anticipated. At a high peak on 7 September, the Blitz continued ceaselessly for the next 76 nights. In one raid, 400 Luftwaffe bombers indiscriminately plunged London and other cities into blazing infernos, killing 43,000 and injuring 139,000 civilians.

Thankfully many of the 13,000 tons of bombs and one million incendiaries failed to explode. Daily, Blaney worked in craters on hushed highways and inside vacated houses to remove an unexploded bomb's fuse. In the dice of life, on 14 November, he was unlucky and the bomb exploded. He was awarded a posthumous George Cross.

Douglas Bader

1940

Douglas Bader, 29 (*fourth from right*), was a legend who won huge admiration – even among Germans. An outstanding sportsman, Bader joined the RAF in 1931 to be acknowledged as an exceptional pilot. Tragedy struck the following year. Bader lost both legs in an air crash. Undaunted, his extraordinary mobility on metal legs turned his defeat of tragedy into inspiration for millions.

After persistent badgering of friends, in June 1940 Bader was appointed commander of 242 Squadron at Coltishall. His sheer flying skills, charm and force of character smothered the doubts of his startled pilots.

In the thrill of the Battle of Britain Bader loved stalking unseen Dorniers; darting out of clouds to pursue stray Messerschmitt 110s over Canterbury with long bursts and then witness them breaking up over the Channel; or, hearing ground control announcing the location of 'Bandit Angels', banking steeply to catch a gaggle of Messerschmitt 109s from below, picking them off like pheasants. Bloodthirsty, he infected his squadron to kill the Hun, shooting down at least 22 enemy aircraft himself and helping his squadron to eliminate another 50. 'Coming in like a lion and going out like a lamb,' he shouted gleefully as the Luftwaffe fled.

But in a reckless dogfight over France, Bader's Spitfire was shot down. He was saved by a parachute, but his metal legs were separated from his body. 'Do you think you could look for my legs?' Bader asked his amazed captors.

With the chivalry of air aces the German fighter pilots invited Bader for tea at their base, and even Goering offered the RAF free passage to deliver a replacement leg to France. Instead, it was parachuted during a bomb raid.

About to be transferred to a POW camp in Germany, Bader lowered himself on fifteen knotted sheets from his hospital window and escaped. While he hid in a Frenchman's house, baffled Germans scoured the countryside seeking a legless pilot. Recaptured, Bader delighted in baiting the Germans. After another attempted escape, he was dispatched to Colditz Castle. Inside his chess set he had concealed 1,000 Reichmarks, three compasses and seven maps. After his fourth abortive escape the Germans confiscated his legs every night.

After liberation in April 1945, he was fêted as a hero and honoured.

In peacetime he worked for Shell and played excellent golf. His example inspired the disabled across the world to 'Reach for the Sky'. He died aged 72, on his way home from celebrating 'Bomber' Harris's 90th birthday.

The Battle of the Atlantic

November 1940

On a sunny evening in early November 1940, Captain Edward Fegen (*left*) from Southsea, Hampshire commanding HMS *Jervis Bay*, a Royal Navy armed merchant cruiser, was protecting thirty-seven merchantmen on an Atlantic crossing. That night, Fegen suddenly encountered the *Admiral Scheer*, a German pocket battleship which days earlier had sunk twenty-one ships of another convoy.

Britain's survival throughout the war depended upon the Battle of the Atlantic – fighting to protect thousands of merchant ships carrying food, oil, raw materials and armaments to the beleaguered island. The threat to those convoys of small merchantmen battling through the heavy Atlantic swell were Germany's surface raiders. These were new, fast, heavily armed cruisers and battleships – and submarines. Unprepared in Autumn 1940 for Germany's warfare, Britain's toll of sunk merchantmen was awesome.

To protect his convoy despite the overwhelming odds from the *Admiral Scheer*, Fegen swung the *Jervis Bay* head-on towards the German battleship aware that his fate was sealed. 'She closed with the raider like a bulldog leaping at a bear,' said an eyewitness. Outgunned during the three-hour battle, the *Jervis Bay*'s bridge was hit by shells, and Fegen's right arm was shattered before his boat finally keeled over and sank, an ensign still fluttering on a splintered mast. Fegen and 200 of his crew drowned with the blazing ship, but his courage allowed the convoy to disperse into the night. Only six ships were finally sunk by the *Admiral Scheer* and thirty-one reached Britain. Fegen was awarded the Victoria Cross for his devotion to duty.

The Dortmund-Ems Canal

12 August 1940

The target on 12 August 1940 for Flight Lieutenant Roderick Learoyd (*above left*) was the Dortmund-Ems Canal, a vital waterway for coal and mineral supplies to Germany's industry, linking the Rhineland, the Ruhr and central Germany.

By night, Learoyd led five Hampdens – slow, technically limited bombers, perilously vulnerable to enemy fire – to attack the canal. In the ill-matched confrontation with German fighters and ack-ack fire, two Hampdens were immediately destroyed and two badly damaged.

Doggedly ignoring the burning dangers, Learoyd flew his Hampden through the glare of searchlights towards the target. As shrapnel repeatedly blasted the fuselage, he dropped his bombs precisely on to the target and miraculously landed his crippled plane back in England.

Although the canal was repaired within two weeks, Learoyd's success and survival was itself awe-inspiring and worthy of a Victoria Cross.

Four years later, on 1 January 1945, 617 Squadron inflicted heavier damage on the canal. During that raid, Flight Sergeant George Thompson (*right*), 25, from Perthshire, was the wireless operator on a Lancaster hit by two shells. As the fire raged in the two gun turrets, Thompson helped the two gunners to safety, and extinguished the flames with his bare hands. As the crippled aircraft crash landed, he survived, only to die of his injuries three weeks later. One of the two gunners lived to be grateful that Thompson's sacrifice was recognized by a Victoria Cross.

The Desert War – General Archibald Wavell

November/December 1940

On 11 November 1940, twenty-one Swordfish of the Fleet Air Arm flew from the carrier *Illustrious* and, in a surprise attack, crippled four major Italian warships, frightening the enemy to move the remaining fleet away from North Africa. For General Archibald Wavell (*far left*) and for Britain it was a remarkable fillip.

Two months earlier, the Italian army had invaded Egypt. Guarding the Suez Canal, the vital link to the Empire, Wavell commanded just 36,000 troops against an Italian army of 600,000. Born in 1883, a tough, one-eyed, outstanding soldier, Wavell responded with a combined air and land counter-attack.

On 9 December, after the blow to the Italian fleet, the British Western Desert Force struck against the Italians at Sidi Barrani. Within two days, five Italian divisions were destroyed in Libya and the strategic fortress of Tobruk captured. At that darkest hour for Britain in Europe, Wavell had delivered a stunning success, transforming North Africa into a major focus of resistance against the Nazis.

Ultra

Reading Germany's most secret communications was the prize most eagerly sought by Britain's leaders. By breaking German codes, they could anticipate and neutralize Hitler's intentions. In 1939, Alan Turing, 27 (*above*), a Cambridge mathematician, was set the task of breaking Germany's unbreakable codes.

Turing arrived at the Government Code and Cypher School, a Victorian mansion at Bletchly Park near Oxford, on 4 September. Around the building, huts were being erected to house the first of several hundred of Britain's most outstanding intellects, especially mathematicians.

By then, Britain had received from Polish and French intelligence officers a vital clue – an Enigma machine used by Germany's military services and their intelligence agencies to encode their messages.

The portable enciphering machine handed to British intelligence was less sophisticated than the latest models in use, but it was sufficient for Turing to understand the challenge.

Working with Gordon Welshman, Turing began calculating a system to beat Enigma's code through a fog of millions of random letters. During 1940 he produced the first results. By 1945, British intelligence could decode the majority of Enigma messages.

The British success in reading the most sensitive German messages throughout the war depended upon keeping that absolutely secret. For the German belief in Enigma's infallibility encouraged its widespread use.

The dissemination of the intercept intelligence was tightly controlled by Group Captain Fred Winterbotham, 43, attached before the war to the Secret Intelligence Service. Under Wintherbotham, the intercepts were classified 'Ultra', identifying their extraordinary importance. Winterbotham delighted in personally delivering the best intercepts to Churchill, since even the knowledge of Enigma's existence was initially restricted to a handful of officers and politicians.

Breaking those German codes was decisive to allied victories in the Atlantic, North Africa, the Mediterranean and Normandy. Remarkably, although by 1945 thousands had become aware of Enigma, the secret was kept for the next 30 years.

Turing's contribution was never officially acknowledged before he committed suicide in June 1954. Winterbotham also received no special recognition. He broke the secret in his 1974 bestseller, *The Ultra Secret*. He died in 1990.

Tobruk

April 1941

In the spring of 1941, all Wavell's successes were wiped out by a new German commander, General Erwin Rommel. Helped by superior weapons and equipment against a ragbag British army depleted by diversions in Greece and Crete, the Afrika Korps stormed towards Cairo and Suez.

Only Tobruk, the grubby fortress guarding North Africa's best harbour and straddling the coastal highway, threatened Rommel's advance to Suez. 'Tobruk must be taken,' ordered Rommel whose armoured units had sent the British forces reeling into retreat.

It was the beginning of the siege of the huge garrison, about the size of the Isle of Wight. From Churchill came the encouraging signal, 'Tobruk is to be held to the death without thought of retirement.'

Under the grilling heat and irritating, baking wind, 34,000 British and Australian soldiers like Corporal John Edmondson, 25 (*above*), from Wagga Wagga, New South Wales, hurriedly dug anti-tank ditches, laid barbed wire and prepared to repel the Germans.

Rommel's attack began on 11 April and stalled the following day amid a blistering sandstorm and a furious fusillade of shells, bombs and bullets from the defenders. During the night of 13/14 April Edmondson was among those counter-attacking a German machine-gun battalion.

In the midst of the furious battle, Edmondson dived to help an officer pinning down an enemy with his bayonet but endangered both by the wounded German and another coming from behind. Edmondson killed both Germans but was himself killed in the close combat. His bravery was rewarded by the Victoria Cross.

At daybreak, Rommel witnessed the carnage. The Allied counter-attack had nearly slaughtered his armoured and artillery battalions. Had the British pressed their attack, Rommel might have been completely routed.

Greece

April 1941

The Allied battle to save Greece from occupation began on 6 April 1941, as the Luftwaffe devastated Belgrade and the Wehrmacht thrust towards Athens. Among the defenders was Sergeant John Hinton, 33 (*below*), The Canterbury Regiment of the New Zealand Division. Realising their weakness, Hinton and the New Zealand division had no alternative but to fight a bitter retreat, as they headed under constant Luftwaffe bombardment towards the beaches in southern Greece for evacuation. But, pinned down by machine-gun fire and shells, Hinton ignored orders to pull back and rushed forward, hurling grenades at the enemy, shooting the machine-gunners and killing several Germans sheltering in a house. The diversion saved his company; but by then it was too late to join the Royal Navy's hazardous Dunkirk-style evacuation of over 50,000 British and Commonwealth servicemen. Instead Hinton fought on until overwhelmed by the Germans and was only captured after receiving a heavy wound. His bravery was rewarded by the Victoria Cross.

Crete

May 1941

Among the 8,400 New Zealanders evacuated from Greece to Crete was Lieutenant Charles Upham, 33, from Christchurch (*right*). Like all the 35,000 soldiers grouped on that mountainous island, Upham was awaiting an imminent German attack. 'We shall aid and maintain the defence of Crete to the utmost,'

pledged Churchill – but no supplies could be spared. The defenders, Churchill urged, were to 'use their bayonets against parachutists'. The island's sole defence until then was the Royal Navy which had ravaged its Italian foe and, at enormous cost of ships and men, was now struggling to resist the German sea and air threat.

Initially, the Allied divisions barred the German invasion, but once German parachutists landed and captured a crucial airport on 20 May, the defenders were pitifully outgunned. By 26 May, Upham had retreated under murderous Luftwaffe bombardment to the port of Sphakia for evacuation. 35,000 Allied troops faced annihilation as nine Royal Navy ships were sunk. Only sacrifices could guarantee anyone's survivial.

Upham selflessly led the charge against advancing German troops. Blown up by one shell, wounded in his foot by another and suffering dysentery, Upham continued the fight, even rescuing a wounded man. In the hours before boarding the last evacuation ships on 30 May, he personally shot 22 Germans. Sailing to Egypt,

leaving behind 3,700 allied dead and 11,300 POWs, Upham could at least reflect upon his own tally towards the 7,000 German dead. In October 1941, Upham formally received his Victoria Cross. Nine months later he was back in action in the Western Desert, hurling grenades and destroying German tanks, guns and vehicles. Even when a machine-gun bullet smashed his arm, he continued leading the charge until he received another wound. His unique bravery was recognized in 1945 by the award of a bar to his Victoria Cross.

Gneisenau

6 April 1941

On a pleasant sunny afternoon in July 1941, a fleet of bombers scattered across England's eastern counties took off towards France for the RAF's biggest-ever daylight raid. Their target was the *Gneisenau* and the *Scharnhorst*, both fast German battle-cruisers which had docked in Brest in March after sinking 22 British ships in the Atlantic. To destroy that colossal threat the RAF was to launch 79 night and 31 daylight raids - a total of 1,161 sorties.

One rushed raid on 6 April 1941 had followed the news that the *Gneisenau* was about to sail. Flying through heavy anti-aircraft flak fired from the ship and the land, Flying Officer Kenneth Campbell (*above*) of 22 Squadron launched a torpedo at point-blank range at the *Gneisenau*'s 6-inch armour plating. The cruiser was damaged below the water-line. But as it swung to return home Campbell's plane was hit and crashed. Campbell was awarded a posthumous Victoria Cross.

Three months later, the damage repaired, another attack was under way. 'On that July afternoon', recalled an RAF pilot, 'the air was as clear as a bell and we could see the French coast half an hour before we reached it.' The clear air also favoured the German fighters massing above the bombers' path.

As the shrapnel and tracer tore into the RAF's obsolete bombers as they cork-screwed to avoid destruction the attack continued, despite gunners and navigators dying in their seats. Over 100 RAF crew perished on that day but both cruisers were sufficiently damaged to keep them in port until February 1942.

Bismarck

May 1941

Hunting the battleships *Bismarck* and *Prinz Eugen* across the North Sea in May 1941 appeared an unequal contest. Although outnumbered by the Royal Navy's five capital ships including the aircraft carrier HMS *Victorious*, the German ships were newer, faster, better armed, more heavily armoured and bigger than any of their British pursuers.

The first engagement started at 5.35am on 24 May. Orange-gold flame belched from HMS *Hood*'s roaring guns as the 42,000-ton battle cruiser engaged the *Bismarck*. Seconds later, the *Bismarck* and *Prinz Eugen* replied and poured shells into the *Hood* as she pushed forward. Black smoke rose from the *Hood* followed by a gigantic explosion. She dis-

integrated and completely disappeared into the depths in just three minutes. 1,338 officers and crew perished leaving just three survivors. The German seamen had proved to be better shots.

At the Admiralty in London there was understandable shock: ten British convoys crossing the Atlantic were in dire risk if Germany's surface raiders escaped to roam the ocean. They committed sixteen more ships to the battle under Admirals Tovey and Somerville.

That evening, the *Bismarck* was lost. Frantic activity found the battleship 36 hours later and Fleet Air Arm Swordfish planes armed with torpedoes were dispatched. Just one torpedo hit the Bismarck's. The great battleship welcomed the dawn on 27 May as the crippled target of the guns from four British capital ships. Within one hour, the pride of the German army was a smoking hulk. 112 of *Bismarck*'s 2,222 crewmen survived.

North Africa: Libya

November 1941

Throughout the autumn of 1941 British and Commonwealth forces in the desert had stealthily prepared for a massive offensive against Rommel's Afrika Korps. Operation Crusader was, in Churchill's opinion, 'The battle [which] will affect the whole course of the war.'

In a bold plan to destroy Rommel's headquarters before the surprise attack, Lieutenant Colonel Geoffrey Keyes (*inset*) and 30 men of Scottish Commando were landed at midnight on 17/18 November by submarine on the coast 250 miles behind enemy lines. After two days hiding in a dry river bed, one group cut the enemy's communications while Keyes led another group to attack Rommel's house.

Silently killing the sentry, Keyes dashed into the house, shot the Germans in the first room and ran firing into a second room. Unfortunately, the Germans inside shot more accurately, killing the 24-year-old from Aberdour, Fifeshire, but were finally silenced by hand grenades, lobbed into the room.

The surviving commandos headed for the beach rendezvous for their escape. Frustrated by bad weather and pursued by the enemy, they dispersed, some finding their way back to British lines, others captured or killed.

Keyes was awarded a Victoria Cross for his gallantry, but his sacrifice was partially in vain. On that night, Rommel was flying back from Rome; and his headquarters had been moved much closer towards Tobruk in preparation for a new offensive.

Among the other victims was Wavell. He was fired by Churchill, furious about the General's weak strategy and his earlier riposte that a big butcher's bill was not necessarily evidence of good tactics.

Libya: Sidi Rezegh

November 1941

Rifleman John Beeley's regiment, the Kings Royal Rifle Corps, had been fighting in a to-and-fro war across the Western desert for months, suffering defeats and retreat, the victims of Rommel's daring tactics, superior equipment and tougher troops.

In the heavy rain early on 18 November, the 22-year-old from Manchester was among 118,000 British and Commonwealth troops attacking the desolate Sidi Rezegh ridge, a 100 foot cliff 20 miles South East of Tobruk. Operation Crusader had taken Rommel's Afrika Korps by complete surprise. Supported by huge accumulated reserves, Beeley's commander, Lieutenant General Sir Alan Cunningham, could expect victory.

As it attacked the enemy's airfield Beeley's company was pinned down by sustained machine-gun and rifle fire. Around him his officers fell wounded, but Beeley, instead of taking cover, pitched forward towards the enemy's positions, firing his Bren gun,

killing two German machine-gunners and an anti-tank gunner before he was shot dead. To his fellow soldiers his sacrifice was an inspiration, spurring them to risk their own lives. The airfield was taken with 700 prisoners.

Surging around the desert in that violent battle, Brigadier John Campbell, 47 *(above)*, commander of the 7th Armoured Division, led his troops from the front, personally firing guns at the Germans, risking the intense fire of artillery, encouraging his men towards victory. But the better German tanks pre-vailed and Campbell died.

In the bitter duel for the ridge, infamously remembered for one day's slaughter of South Africans as the 'Sunday of the Dead', British and Commonwealth fatalities escalated to 17,700. The sacrifice of Campbell and Beeley reflected poorly on the inexperienced Lieutenant General Cunningham who lost his nerve and was fired. Rommel recap-tured the ridge on 1 December.

Awarded the Victoria Cross, both Beeley and Campbell were buried near to where they fell.

Tobruk

November 1941

For more than seven months Tobruk had been besieged. 'It seems unthinkable,' signalled Churchill, that the fortress of Tobruk should be abandoned.' Enduring ceaseless sniper fire, shelling and air attacks, the defenders, the Desert Rats gradually descended into holes for their survival not only from the enemy but also from the blistering sun, insects and the sand.

During the early hours of 21 November, the Tobruk garrison broke out into the desert to join Operation Crusader, Churchill's bid to destroy Rommel's Afrika Korps. 'The only thing that matters,' wrote Churchill, 'is to beat the the life out of Rommel & Co.'

In the swirling dust and the blazing sun, officers and men risked their lives to save their comrades.

Among them was Captain Philip Gardner, 27 (*left*), of the Royal Tank Regiment. Seeing that a fellow officer had lost both legs in a crippled armoured car, Gardner ignored both the persistent danger of superior German anti-tank guns and his wounds, to bring his fellow officer to safety. His bravery was recognized by a Victoria Cross.

In the meantime, Captain James Jackman, 25 (*right*), of the Royal Northumberland Fusiliers was attacking El Duda, a hill held by the Germans. Under the very field glasses of Rommel, Jackman led a machine-gun company to assault the ridge weaving through charred tanks and corpses draped over destroyed guns. In the frantic battle, later joined by Rommel to prevent his forces becoming 'the meat in the sandwich', Jackman coolly inspired his men to press forward until he was killed and posthumously awarded a Victoria Cross. The battle was won by Rommel.

Churchill Amid the Ruins

Defeats in France, Greece, Crete, North Africa and in the Atlantic bore heavily on Churchill as he surveyed the devastation caused to Britain's cities by the Luftwaffe. The cheers of Englishmen when they saw the Prime Minister reduced him, in private, to tears. 'They have such confidence. It is a grave responsibility,' he confessed to his intimate staff.

Until December 1941, Britain stood alone in Western Europe and North Africa against Hitler. Germany's invasion of the Soviet Union in June had relieved the pressure, the nightmare in the Atlantic had been relieved by 'Ultra' but the threat in the Middle East and Mediterranean appeared unbeatable. In November, the *Ark Royal*, an aircraft carrier, was sunk by a U-boat.

Against the odds, Churchill symbolized the nation's defiance. 'We are at the utmost strain,' lamented the Prime Minister. Deliverance came with the Japanese attack on Pearl Harbor on 7 December (*below*) and Germany's declaration of war against the United States. 'We are all in the same boat now,' President Roosevelt told Churchill.

Malta

1941

By late 1941, the Royal Navy's single base in the central Mediterranean was the island of Malta, a beacon for British convoys hazarding the perilous waters en route to Egypt. From there, British planes, ships and submarines could cut into the lines of communication and oil supply essential to the fate of the Afrika Korps and the Axis navies and airforces launched an intense air bombardment and blockade of the island from nearby Sicily.

After the first attacks during 1941, they intensified to a daily bombardment from 1 January 1942 until 24 July. As the population moved underground, more bombs dropped on Malta than on London in the Blitz. In these conditions, the health of the 270,000 islanders sharply deteriorated – there were outbreaks of malnutrition, scabies and typhoid, and nearly 1,500 were killed. After a lull, the German offensive recommenced and thirty-one ships were sunk. Food and fuel supplies dwindled before relief came after Rommel's defeat in November 1942.

For withstanding the horrendous punishment the island was awarded the George Cross.

The Nerve Centre of Government

'I spent the whole war in the middle of a web,' testified General Sir Hastings Ismay (*below*), the indispensable chief of staff for Churchill.

A war leader's success depends on the efficiency of his machinery of government. Having appointed himself Minister of Defence, Churchill centralized the management of the war from Downing Street and the underground Cabinet Office. One section of Churchill's office was organized to fight the war and the other to supervise supplies. At weekends Churchill moved to Chequers, inviting his staff to discuss strategy in the countryside. For nearly five years, Ismay was responsible for oiling that machinery, travelling with Churchill to America, North Africa and Russia.

Malaya

1942

Even in humiliation, bravery is recognized. In the aftermath of the surprise Japanese invasion of Malaya on 7 and 8 December 1941, Lieutenant Colonel Arthur Cumming, 46 *(below left)*, the commander of the 2/12th Frontier Force regiment of the Indian Army, was sent north from Singapore to defend Kuantan, on the South China Sea. Off the coast, *Repulse* and *Prince of Wales*, two of the Royal Navy's most powerful warships, had just been sunk by Japanese fighters, drowning 840 crew.

Although the Allied forces under the command of Lieutenant General Arthur Percival outnumbered the Japanese, the odds were weighted in the invader's favour. Cumming's Indian soldiers were poorly trained – some had never seen a tank in their lives – and were swept aside in a furious onslaught by the battle-hardened Japanese.

Yet Cumming led a small group in a counter attack. Wounded twice in the stomach by bayonets, he gained sufficient time for his battalion to regroup, collect the wounded, and withdraw. Considering the bad judgment of General Percival, Cumming's actions were sufficiently heroic to be awarded the Victoria Cross.

Worse followed. After returning to Singapore, on 15 February, Cumming and 85,000 other Allied troops were ordered by the uninspiring and limp Percival not to counter-attack the 35,000 vulnerable Japanese to defeat.

Cumming survived captivity, and became a superintendent of police in Cyprus in the 1950s, and fought the Eoka terrorists.

POWS of the Japanese

Captain Douglas Ford, 25, The Royal Scots, was taken prisoner by the Japanese in Hong Kong in December 1941, and witnessed the grotesque inhumanity of his captors. All over the island, innocent civilians were being mutilated, tortured and murdered. Even in the hospital patients were bayonetted in beds or in the operating theatre. Across the territory women were raped and beheaded. For the victors, murder was a sport and mutilation a pastime.

Ford began plotting an escape with Colonel Lance Newnham, 44, of The Middlesex Regiment. Eventually their plan was discovered and the Japanese demanded the names of their accomplices. Despite the most vile torture, both remained silent until they were executed.

A similar fate befell John Fraser, 46, an assistant attorney general. Despite prolonged torture, he too refused to betray his fellow prisoners and was executed.

All three were awarded the George Cross.

The Defence of the Atlantic

Admiral Sir Dudley Pound, Admiral of the Fleet, plotted the defence of Royal Navy and British merchant ships. Constantly overworked but dedicated, Pound masterminded the development of tactics to defeat the U-boats in the Atlantic, the sinking of the *Bismarck* and the destruction or neutralization of Germany's remaining surface raiders.

When Admiral Sir Max Horton (*above*), became commander of the Western approaches in 1942, he inherited a strong force of reconnaisance aircraft of Coastal Command, a small but successful pack of submarines, a deft planning organization for the safe passage of convoys and invaluable intelligence from 'Ultra'.

Vera Lynn

Born in East Ham, the daughter of a docker, Vera Lynn was the 'girl next door' for whom British troops felt they were fighting. With her song in 1939, 'We'll Meet Again', she was voted the 'Forces' Sweetheart'. As the friendly presenter of the wartime show 'Sincerely Yours', she passed messages of love and memories between servicemen in the desert or jungle and their families at home followed by simple, sincere and sentimental songs.

Like many ENSA women, entertaining the troops, Vera Lynn travelled across the Middle East and Far East to meet 'her boys'. 'They would come out of the jungle and sit on the grass and listen, and then get up and go back with their tommy-guns and rifles over their shoulders.'

Prinz Eugen

12 February 1942

In the morning mist on 12 February, the cruisers *Gneisenau*, *Scharnhorst* and *Prinz Eugen* began sailing through the Straits of Dover. They had sailed from Brest at midnight, breaking a year-long blockade to prevent their escape out into the Atlantic.

Admiralty intelligence had anticipated their passage to Germany but, despite a close watch on Brest, the Royal Navy was taken by surprise by the affront of the three capital ships daring to sail up the English Channel in daylight. Unknown to the Admiralty, German scientists had perfected counter-radar measures which that day had jammed and neutralized British radar defences along the South coast.

When finally the German armada was spotted at 11 am, the gamut of British shore batteries, air and sea forces was hurled against the three goliaths and their escorts.

Taking off from Manston, Kent, six torpedo-carrying Swordfish led by Lieutenant Commander Eugene Esmonde, 32 (*above*), of 825 Squadron, Fleet

Air Arm, sped towards the flotilla. Within minutes, the lumbering squadron's escort was engaged by aggressive Luftwaffe fighters and soon the Swordfish were battered by relentless enemy fire. Coolly, despite his plane suffering a direct hit, Esmonde continued his attack, releasing his torpedo, but was unable to prevent his burning plane crashing into the sea. He and the five other pilots were all killed. For his courage he was rewarded with the Victoria Cross.

More waves of RAF bombers and Royal Navy destroyers firing torpedoes proved unable to hit the cruisers. The only damage to the *Scharnhorst* and *Gneisenau* was caused by mines which had been dropped from the air.

Two weeks later in Kiel harbour, the *Gneisenau* was hit by RAF bombers and permanently decommissioned.

The *Scharnhorst*, having sheltered in a Norwegian fjord, was finally engaged at Christmas, 1943 by three Royal Navy cruisers under Admiral Robert Burnett. Brilliant seamanship by Burnett spelled the *Scharnhorst*'s doom within one day. It sank into the Norwegian Sea.

The St Nazaire Raid

27 March 1942

Commander Robert 'Red' Ryder's (*near right*) mission on the night of 27/28 March 1942 was audacious and unusual. The 34-year-old Londoner was (with Lieutenant Commander Stephen Beattie, *centre*) to sail HMS *Campbeltown* flying the Swastika through German defences into St Nazaire, the French Atlantic port. Concealed on board were 268 British commandos under the command of Lieutenant Colonel Augustus Newman. Their mission, code-named Operation Chariot, was to destroy the dry dock and prevent its use by the German battleship *Tirpitz*.

Amid a spectacular exchange of fire at close range, Ryder rammed the destroyer carrying five tons of explosives into the dock gates while Newman, boldly leading from the front, directed six Commando units to jump down onto the dockside, killing hordes of German defenders while demolition teams laid charges among the port's installations.

As the explosives in the harbour and on board HMS *Campbeltown* detonated, successfully destroying the targets, the surviving commandos hastened towards the remnants of a flotilla of craft prepared for their evacuation. Loaded with the wounded, the motor launches and gun boats sped towards open sea pursued by the Germans. On board two craft, Sergeant Thomas Durrant and Able Seaman William Savage (*far right*) stubbornly continued firing a Lewis gun and a pom-pom at the enemy. Unprotected and each of them wounded, they refused to surrender until each were killed.

All the five men named were awarded the Victoria Cross. 78 others were decorated. Only 270 of the 630 participants returned to England; 144 died; the remainder, including Colonel Newman, were captured. Newman became a leading engineer and died in 1972. Ryder became a member of parliament and was buried at sea in 1986.

Sir Charles Portal – Bomber Command HQ

Driven out of Europe and relentlessly bombarded by the Luftwaffe, Churchill's ambition to revenge the widespread destruction of British cities and strike at the heart of Germany could only be carried out by Bomber Command.

That task fell to Air Vice-Marshal Sir Charles Portal, an RAF officer since 1915, appointed Chief of Bomber Command in April 1940 and soon after promoted to Chief of the Air Staff. Portal's initial plan to bomb only Germany's strategic installations was frustrated by an unfortunate reality: the RAF was suffering from inadequate technical equipment to fly their planes to a target and drop bombs precisely.

Churchill's new directive was explicit: make the German people suffer as the people of London,

Coventry and Birmingham had suffered. Battering the Reich from the air, until the invasion of occupied Europe, reminded Hitler that Britain was undefeated. The blanket bombing of German cities and civilians, Portal agreed with Churchill, was the only available weapon to undermine the German citizens' faith in the Nazis, destroy the Reich's industrial might and terrorize the enemy.

Brave crewmen, flying dangerously obsolete aircraft over Germany were soon being killed for only meagre results. Despite that failure and despite Churchill's increasing scepticism over the effectiveness of the bombing, Portal insisted that the RAF could deliver the knock-out blow.

History would question Portal's judgment, but eventually he delivered what was required by the politicians and public in the turbulence of war. Bomber Command's critics could predict neither Germany's fate had the war not been taken to the heart of its cities, nor the additional cost in Allied lives.

Sir Archibald McIndoe FRCS - The Guinea Pig Club

As Flight Lieutenant Tom Gleave led the attack on a formation of Ju 88 bombers over the south coast, his Hurricane was hit. 'A long spout of flame curled up from the starboard wing, up the cockpit and across my right shoulder. I had some crazy notion that if I rocked the aircraft the fire might go out. Instead, the flames increased until the cockpit was like the centre of a blow-lamp nozzle.' A great flash and explosion blew Gleave out of the cockpit. Pulling the parachute ripcord, he floated down. Fire had consumed his nose, shrivelling the nostrils into tiny holes between his eyes. His hands, arms and legs were burned so badly he could no longer use them.

Gleave's salvation was Dr Archibald McIndoe. Born in 1900 in New Zealand, McIndoe was a plastic surgeon who rebuilt the faces and bodies of mutilated fliers. In Ward 3 of a brown wooden hut behind the Queen Victoria Cottage Hospital in East Grinstead, he and his team gave hope and a new life to Gleave and many others fried beyond recognition.

For Gleave, McIndoe built a new nose; for others, he rebuilt entire faces, eyes, ears, limbs and more. He also encouraged their mental rehabilitation, helping them to come to terms with their terrifying appearance.

Wives, girlfriends and servicewomen were asked to meet the Guinea Pigs, as the men were known, at special dances. Although they recoiled in horror at first sight, the women were mindful of the men's plight. 'I gritted my teeth,' recalled ATS Vera Cole, 'walked straight up to one of them and began to talk. Other girls followed my example. Soon their scarred hands and faces faded into the background.' Thanks to McIndoe, Gleave and the other courageous young men could rebuild their lives.

McIndoe was knighted in 1947 – one of many honours he received before he died in 1960.

Bombing Cologne

May 1942

The task of damaging the image of German invincibility in the harsh days of 1942 rested upon Bomber Command. The young pilots and crew, flying slow, vulnerable planes, kept alive the morale of the British people and the politicians' promise that Hitler would be defeated in Germany itself.

Britain's imagination was sparked on 30 May 1942 by the first '1,000 bomber raid' against Cologne – the biggest concentration of air power in history. Even the Nazi leaders gasped.

Flying Officer Leslie Manser, 20 (*right*), was among the last of the 1,046 pilots to take off from airfields scattered across England that moonlit night. Flying a Manchester, an old, underpowered bomber, it was his fourteenth mission.

Like so many young men of Bomber Command, Manser had left the serene beauty of the English countryside knowing that within hours he would be over Germany avoiding flak and fighting enemy fighters, hoping that luck and skill would save him from a gruesome death. As they neared Cologne, Manser blinked hard at the vast red glow – a city already ablaze, amok and devastated.

At the right moment, Manser began his approach towards the inferno. Suddenly a searchlight glared into the cockpit, swiftly followed by anti-aircraft shells which punctured the metal and tore the controls. Ignoring the growing mayhem, Manser continued his run, dropped his bombs and turned for home. More shells ripped through the fuselage as he struggled to lose the searchlights and douse the fires before the fuel exploded. He ordered his crew to hurl everything possible outside to lighten the load.

His struggle to fly home and avoid capture was soon lost. 'Prepare to abandon aircraft,' called Manser. As his four crew bailed out, Manser gripped the controls to prevent the aircraft spiralling out of control and killing everyone. Alone, he landed on a ploughed field but seconds later an explosion ripped through the aircraft. Ablaze, he struggled out defiantly, dragged himself to a tree and died knowing he had saved the lives of his crew. He was one of 50,000 air crew of Bomber Command who lost their lives during the war. Manser was awarded the Victoria Cross.

Dieppe

19 August 1942

Risking one's life in a forlorn battle is an awful fate. Like over 6,000 other British, Canadian and Ameri-can servicemen, Captain Patrick Porteous, 24 (*right*), of the Royal Regiment of Artillery attached to the Commandos, was unaware as he approached the French Channel port of Dieppe by sea on 19 August 1942 that 'Operation Jubilee' was destined to be calamitous.

Bowing to intense pressure from home and abroad, Churchill had agreed to a massive raid against the German positions. But in the weeks before, Bomber Command had refused to attack the area and the Admiralty had withheld battleships for fire support.

As the landing craft headed towards the beaches, those fatal weaknesses were compounded by the absence of intelligence about hidden German gun emplacements or the whereabouts of German command posts. Even the advantage of surprise was lost when the task force was spotted in the Channel by a German convoy known to be in the area.

As the Allied troops struggled up the beaches and cliffs, the cost of that abysmal planning was slaughter on a monumental scale. One exception were 250

British Commandos whose individual planning and execution were meticulous.

Captain Porteous's target was a gun emplacement. Racing through the French countryside under withering enemy fire for the rest of the night, he saw his superiors fall and, although wounded himself, took command as his target loomed. Through detonating smoke bombs, Porteous led the mad rush, shooting one German dead and leading a bayonet and bombing charge against the remaining German gunners. As the demolition charges exploded, the Commandos successfully rejoined their landing craft, carrying their wounded. Porteous was awarded a Victoria Cross.

Along the coast, the torn bodies and blood on the beaches were testament to a different fate. Under constant fire, the Royal Navy withdrew to save its craft, abandoning over 1,000 dead and leaving many of the 2,500 wounded and more than 2,000 others to surrender. Witnessing that tragedy from a departing landing craft, the Hon Captain John Foote, the Canadian chaplain who had ministered for eight hours to the wounded and dying on the beaches, coolly disembarked and sacrificed his journey to safety. He deliberately surrendered to the Germans so that he could care for those who would spend the war as POWs – a gallant act recognized by the Victoria Cross.

Admiral Sir Andrew Cunningham

The mastermind of the Battle of the Mediterranean was Sir Andrew B. Cunningham (*inset*), born in 1883. Known by his initials, 'ABC', Cunningham's experience in the Navy since 1897 lay behind his brilliant achievements: mauling the Italian fleet in Taranto and Matapan in 1940; organizing the evacuation from Crete in 1941; helping plan the Allied landings in North Africa in 1942; protecting the lifeline of supplies for the Allied armies in the desert; and frustrating German attempts to evacuate their armies from North Africa. In reply to a staff complaint during the evacuation from Crete that fighting the Luftwaffe was akin to butting one's head against a wall, Cunningham replied, 'What you have forgotten, you miserable undertaker, is that you may be loosening a brick.'

His cool approach in adversity, despite horrendous losses caused by German aircraft and submarines, was crucial to the Allied armies defeat of Rommel in the desert and to their campaign in Italy. 'Sink, burn, destroy. Let nothing pass,' was his order in 1943.

After the Allied landings in Sicily and Italy in 1943, Cunningham confronted the Italian fleet and, on 11 September, memorably signalled the Admiralty in London: 'Be pleased to inform their Lordships that the Italian battle fleet now lies at anchor under the guns of the Fortress of Malta.' He died in 1963.

British Submarine Warfare

1939-1943

The most potent force against the German and Italian convoys in the Mediterranean replenishing their armies in North Africa was the 10th Flotilla of small British submarines based in Malta. Blessed with names like *Unseen*, *Unrivalled*, *Unbeaten*, *Unique*, *Utmost*, *Upright* and *Upholder*, the crews were guided by intercepts from 'Ultra' to attack.

On the evening of 25 May 1941, Lieutenant Commander Malcolm Wanklyn, 31 (*above*), of HM Submarine *Upholder*, operating south of Sicily saw through his periscope four heavily protected troop ships. *Upholder* had already been in action and only two torpedoes remained. Evading the destroyers, Wanklyn aimed and hit the *Conte Rosse*, causing 1,200 deaths and bringing his tally for that mission

to 140,000 tons of enemy shipping. His success was greeted by thirty-seven depth charges within twenty minutes. Evading capture and death, Wanklyn returned to Malta to be awarded the Victoria Cross. Within a year, he died on operation in the Gulf of Tripoli. His widow received his medal from King George Vl at Buckingham Palace.

A similar fate befell Commander John Linton, 38, from Monmouthshire. Under Linton's command, HM Submarine *Turbulent* sank approximately 100,000 tons of shipping, including a cruiser, a destroyer, a U-boat and twenty-eight other ships. He even destroyed three trains by gunfire. In 1943, his last year, Commander Linton spent 254 days at sea, submerged for nearly half the time. His submarine survived thirteen pursuits and approximately 250 depth charges but never returned from a mission inside the Italian harbour of Maddelina. He too won a posthumous Victoria Cross.

The Mediterranean War - Bomb Disposal

February 1942

Victory in the desert was possible only if the Royal Navy controlled the Mediterranean Sea. Protecting British supply lines across the Mediterranean to the 8th Army, to the Suez Canal and to India and Singapore, and preventing Italian and German merchant ships delivering weapons and oil to Rommel, was a fierce and prolonged battle.

Protecting British convoys and attacking German and Italian ships had proved costly. In late 1941, the aircraft carrier *Ark Royal*, three battleships and a cruiser had been damaged or sunk by the enemy. Those defeats allowed Rommel to assemble a powerful army.

In February 1942, a peak in the naval war, the British Army's survival depended upon a handful of British submarines like the *Thrasher*.

Using intelligence from Ultra, *Thrasher* attacked and sank an enemy supply ship, dived to escape but was attacked. Hours later, when the danger had passed, the submarine surfaced, revealing two unexploded bombs wedged into the outside casing.

Few acts of courage require more cool headedness than defusing a live bomb, but Lieutenant Peter Roberts, 25, from Buckinghamshire (*left*), and Petty Officer Thomas Gould, 28, from Dover (*right*), fearlessly threw one bomb overboard and then spent forty minutes cradling the second bomb out of its confined space before it too could be deposited in the depths. Both were awarded the Victoria Cross.

The Desert

July 1942

For the British, the news that Tobruk and 35,000 troops had surrendered on 20 June 1942 was, wrote Churchill, 'one of the heaviest blows I can recall during the war'. The loss of men and of vast supplies of oil and trucks was a disgrace which devastated the British Army's morale and reputation. Even Churchill was censured in Parliament – and he blamed Rommel!

Yet even as Rommel, promoted to Field Marshal, was poised to launch his final assault on Cairo on 1 July, a ferocious Allied counter-offensive stunned his troops.

Individual soldiers like Private Arthur Gurney, 34, from Day Dawn, Western Australia (*right*), dis-played the courage upon which any future victory must depend.

Charging across the sand dunes on 22 July and lurching into one machine gun-post, Gurney bayonetted three Italians, then charged another post, killing two more Italians.

Only as he stormed a third was he killed by a grenade. As the enemy battalion surrendered, Gurney's body was found and the value of his heroic deed recognized.

Further across the desert, Sergeant Keith Elliot, 26, from Apiti, New Zealand (*left*), had led his platoon through heavy machine-gun and mortar fire to charge the German positions with bayonets drawn, capturing four enemy posts and 130 POWs.

Yet once again, their valour – recognized by the Victoria Cross – was not immediately rewarded. The following day, 23 July, Rommel toasted victory, having destroyed over 200 British tanks.

Montgomery in the Desert

Autumn 1942

The arrival of Lieutenant General Bernard Montgomery, 45, in Egypt in August 1942 sparked an immediate improvement in morale: 'Kill the Germans wherever you find them.'

Incisive, utterly dedicated and meticulous, but also unpleasant, conceited and cruel, Montgomery had been commissioned in the Royal Warwickshire Regiment, was wounded in the First World War and thereafter devoted himself to soldiering and war. Having performed well during the battle for France in 1940, his promotion relied on others' misfortune rather than on inevitability.

In North Africa, Montgomery's advantages over his enemy were new tanks, fresh supplies and Ultra.

Nearly all Rommel's coded, top secret messages were placed on Montgomery's desk within hours of despatch.

On 23 October, knowing that Rommel was on leave in Germany, Montgomery launched his first offensive. His personal message to his troops on the eve of Alamein was not an exaggeration: 'The battle which is now about to begin will be one of the decisive battles of history. It will be the turning-point of the war. The eyes of the whole world will be on us, watching anxiously which way the battle will swing. We can give them their answer at once it will swing our way.'

Among those leading the charge was Sergeant William Kirby, 40 (*inset right*), born in County Durham but living in Australia. Hurling himself that night into a machine-gun post, he killed three and captured twelve.

During the next seven days, as the German troops, deprived of gasoline, recoiled in front of overwhelming numbers, Kirby and his fellow Australians under General Morshead swarmed over 500,000 mines, regardless of rapid German fire. By 30 October, more than 10,000 Allied soldiers had died as the Australians finally wedged into Rommel's sector. Among those magnificent fighters was Sergeant Kirby, killed throwing grenades at well fortified enemy positions. The following day, Rommel engaged in his last great desert battle at El Alamein and then ordered the retreat. Kirby was awarded the Victoria Cross.

Montgomery's pride in victory was flashed to his superiors: 'I obtained complete surprise... It's been a terrific party ... and so far Rommel has had to dance completely to my tune.'

The chase would continue for over 2,000 miles.

The Desert Air War

November/December 1942

After El Alamein, the British and Commonwealth armies, outstripped by superior German tanks and guns in the desert war, relied upon RAF fighters and bombers to harass and destroy the enemy.

Day and night, RAF pilots flew from desert airfields, targeting enemy concentrations and moving vehicles. Twice during that war, Rommel himself barely survived heavy bombs and machine-gun fire from a diving fighter.

Among those fighting for air superiority was Wing Commander Hugh Malcolm, 25 (*inset above left*), from Dundee, Scotland whose light bombers of 18

Squadron destroyed tons of enemy supplies, marauded German positions and finally challenged the enemy's air force based in Libya.

Like so many pilots, surviving on the brink of attrition and knowing that as each mission was completed his odds for survival shortened, Malcolm met his end on 4 December, overwhelmed by a swarm of enemy fighters. His posthumous Victoria Cross rewarded months of endurance and danger by both himself and his fellow officers who also died in blazing aircraft hurtling towards the desert unable to escape the inferno.

Colonel David Stirling

Driving deep behind enemy lines through the North African desert in the fifteen months after October 1941, Colonel David Stirling, 26, nicknamed 'the Phantom Major' by the Germans, delighted in the mayhem and destruction caused by his élite regiment, the 1st Special Air Service.

Blowing up parked aircraft, derailing trains, incinerating petrol dumps and hijacking lorries, Stirling's raiders operated under the motto 'Who Dares Wins'. Rommel, who was deceived that SAS was a substantial airborne force, blamed Stirling for causing more damage than any other group of that size. According to Montgomery, 'The boy Stirling is quite mad. However in war there is a place for mad people.'

Standing 6 feet 5 inches tall, with an equally big personality, but remarkably deft in movement, Lieutenant Stirling had gatecrashed British headquarters in Cairo in July 1941 to win approval to build SAS from the remnants of a British commando force. Only the fearless qualified to join his group. Instead of parachuting to a target they drove long distances and, arriving at night, laid time bombs underneath aircraft or careered down runways shooting bursts at the parked Luftwaffe bombers and fighters. In one spectacular raid, forty-seven aircraft were destroyed. Their total tally was 350 aircraft.

Captured by German troops in 1943, Stirling's wartime career was terminated. After four attempted escapes he was interned in Colditz. In his absence, SAS was replaced by a Special Boat Squadron, which wreaked havoc in the Mediterranean and was but then re-formed for the Normandy invasion, in which it performed outstandingly.

Awarded a DSO, Stirling was probably the most undecorated hero of the war, but he lived to enjoy the legend and the formation of the SAS Regiment, which served as a model for all other countries. He died in 1990.

Gubbins

Unconventional warfare had few better champions than Major General Colin Gubbins, 47 (*below*), from the Western Isles of Scotland, who in 1943 became executive director of the Special Operations Executive (SOE). Established with Churchill's blessing to 'set Europe ablaze', SOE's task was to support, organize and arm Europe's underground and resistance movements.

The secret armies' successes throughout occupied Europe depended upon Gubbins' energy and his understanding of irregular warfare and the special qualities required of combatants. Author of *The Art of Guerrilla Warfare*, his unusual service record provided shrewd expertise.

After fighting the Bolsheviks in Russia in 1919, he operated against the Irish Nationalists until 1922. He then served as an intelligence officer in India at the beginning of that country's unrest, before travelling through Poland in 1939 to plan subversive warfare against the Germans. His first operations in Norway in 1940 were to organize stay-behind guerrillas to harass the Germans by sabotage and subversion.

After the fall of France, Gubbins' understanding of intelligence and his gift of diplomacy managed and inspired a collection of international intellectuals, professionals, artists and traders joining SOE to understand and obey the rules of operating in enemy territory. Thanks to his enthusiasm and commitment, he gave SOE spirit and substance and a blueprint for turning an amateur group into an organized army.

SOE's recruits, trained in the Highlands and at Beaulieu, were dispatched only after exhaustive training in combat, survival, spy tradecraft, radio communications and sabotage. Under Gubbins' supervision, radio equipment was improved and the opportunities for sabotage enhanced with the invention of plastic explosives.

Gubbins was awarded the KCMG, DSO and MC. He retired to Scotland after SOE's disbandment in 1946.

Odette Sansom GC, OBE

1942

Born in France, 30 year-old Odette Sansom (*above with her daughters*), alias 'Lise', left three young daughters in Britain to land by felucca in France in 1942. Among the first of over fifty women sent by SOE to France, she was to be the courier for Peter Churchill, an enthusiastic SOE officer, not related to the Prime Minister.

The problems for SOE agents were considerable. Churchill was a liaison officer for a number of large resistance networks, battling first with SOE headquarters to secure planes to parachute weapons and explosives to the networks; and secondly to persuade the French resistants to engage in sabotage rather than internecine arguments. Fearful that the disputes among the resistance groups had endangered their own secu-

rity, Churchill and Odette moved near to Geneva but soon a Gestapo interrogation extracted their identity and location. SOE's security procedures had collapsed and both Churchill and Odette were arrested.

Odette's salvation was her quickwitted 'confession' that she was related to the famous Prime Minister. The Gestapo, sensing the possibility of a future pawn of influence, decided her life was of potential value.

Transported to Ravensbrück concentration camp, she was incarcerated until the end of the war in solitary confinement in darkness, often without food, adjacent to an execution ground.

On 3 May 1945, Ravensbrück's commandant, Fritz Suhren, drove Odette in his superb Mercedes-Benz car to the American lines hoping she would plead for his life. The mass murderer's expectations were shortlived. He was executed and Odette awarded the George Cross. She died in 1995.

Colditz - Airey Neave

Among the 50,000 British troops captured in France in 1940 were some who had no intention of vegetating for years in German POW camps. Even among those spirited few, Lieutenant Airey Neave, 24 (*below*), was exceptional. After his first escape and recapture, Neave was dispatched to Colditz, an impregnable, medieval castle perched high on a rock precipice, surrounded by a moat and guarded by sentries with machine-guns. Colditz was the prison for the élite of escapers, deemed by the Germans to be an invulnerable cage for the 'bad boys'.

But inevitably, Colditz's inhabitants were preoccupied with plans to embarrass their captors, alias 'the Goons'.

Neave rose to the challenge. Escape, in his opinion, required 'a man equipped with more than a compass, maps, papers, disguise and a plan, but with an inner confidence, a serenity of spirit which makes him a Pilgrim.'

By summer 1941, using the unique talents of other prisoners, Neave had obtained forged identity papers, real German money and, most importantly, assembled a fake German army uniform from dyed fabrics with attached insignia, including a swastika made of painted linoleum and a bayonet carved of wood.

On the evening of 5 January 1942, Neave and Tony Luteyn, a Dutch POW, dressed as Prussian officers and greeting German sentries, walked steadily past the castle's gatehouse, over the moat bridge into the snow-covered forest. Dumping their German clothes, the two POWs hurried to the railway station to travel through Nazi Germany to Switzerland.

At 5am, disguised as Dutch labourers, Neave and Luteyn were mingling with German workers. Over the next days, they travelled in a train compartment with an SS officer, were nearly arrested twice and, finally, struggled through freezing snowdrifts towards the Swiss border. As the German sentry unwittingly turned away, they grappled across the snow to freedom. Stopped by a Swiss policeman, Neave disclosed their identity. 'Then Luteyn, the guard with his rifle on his shoulder and I clasped each others' hands and danced in the snow... The guard shouted merrily as if he was the most delighted man in the world that we had escaped the tyranny of Hitler.' Travelling on false papers through France, Spain and Gibraltar, Neave reached England in May.

In July 1944, Neave returned to France and the next year was appointed to the International Military Tribunal at Nuremberg. In 1953 he was elected Conservative MP for Abingdon. In 1979 he was murdered within the precinct of the Houses of Parliament by an IRA bomb.

The Cockleshell Heroes

December 1942

HM Submarine *Tuna* surfaced at midnight on 7 December 1942 just beyond the French port of Bordeaux. Captain HG 'Blondie' Hasler (*inset, in bow of canoe*) and nine Royal Marine Commandos – armed, black-faced and camouflaged – slipped into five canoes and began paddling towards the river Gironde. In each canoe were weapons and limpet mines. After six months' intensive training, their task was to penetrate the port, attach the mines to anchored ships, and return to Britain with the help of the French resistance.

As the ten paddled furiously through the freezing sea, the canoes or cockles encountered heavy tides. One cockle was lost, another overturned and then a third disappeared. Only Hasler and three others struggled ashore and hid themselves during the day. On 11 December the four reached Bordeaux.

That night, hugging sixteen limpets fused to explode nine hours later, the Commandos slipped into the port's dark waters. While sentries stomped on the brightly lit decks high above, the Commandos silently attached their magnetic mines to the biggest ships. Their work completed, the cockles were scuttled and the two teams parted to make their way home. By then sixteen bombs had exploded. Hasler and his companion travelled through Spain and arrived in London five months later. Of their comrades, one had drowned and seven others had been caught and executed, victims of a war crime. Since their bravery was not witnessed by a senior officer, no medals were awarded. But the Cockleshell Heroes were remembered and honoured in an emotional feature film.

North Africa: Monty's Trap

March 1943

During February 1943, the Allied advance into Tunisa had stalled while Montgomery regrouped and waited for supplies. On 6 March Rommel attacked at Medenine. 'It's an absolute gift and the man must be mad,' laughed Montgomery as the Germans were slaughtered in his trap. Rommel retired to Germany as Montgomery launched an offensive up the coast towards the fortified Mareth line manned by Italians supported by German panzers.

When battle began on the night of 20/21 March, Lieutenant Colonel Derek Seagrim, 40 (*above*), commander of the 7th Battalion, the Green Howards, moved forward against the concrete pillboxes, barbed wire and anti-tank ditches – obstacles more severe than had been expected.

For some moments the intensity of the Italian fire destabilized the attack, but with a pistol in his hand and shouting 'Come on, Green Howards,' Seagrim led his men towards the ditch, was the first on to the scaling ladder and led the capture of two machine-gun posts. Under heavy fire, he pressed on to capture another machine-gun post before he was killed. His company, after another reverse, won victory seven days later.

Seagrim, from Bournemouth, was awarded the Victoria Cross. His brother, Major Hugh Seagrim, was posthumously awarded the George Cross for his courage in Burma, where he was brutally executed by the Japanese.

North Africa: Victory

April 1943

In April 1943, the German and Italian armies were in retreat towards Bizerta on the Tunisian coast chased across the Eastern Dorsale desert by, among others, Lieutenant Colonel Lorne Campbell, 41 (*left*), commanding 7 Battalion, the Argyll and Sutherland Highlanders in Montgomery's 8th Army.

In previous weeks Campbell had fallen back under a German counter-attack, but after 19 March he was among those racing to recapture the terrain – towards the decisive battle at Wadi Akarit.

On 6 April, in darkness, Campbell moved forward to break through another enemy minefield and anti-tank ditch. Success would allow the 8th Army's advance to continue. Campbell crossed the danger zone, attacked the German positions and took 600 POWs. At daybreak, the counter-attack began. Amid murderous gunfire and bombardment, Campbell kept his men steady, repulsing attacks, and finally held his bridge-head, allowing the 8th Army to break through Wadi

Akarit. Campbell, from The Airds in Argyllshire, won the Victoria Cross for his outstanding leadership.

In that break-out, Lord Lyell, 30, Captain in the Scots Guards from London (*far left*), led four NCOs, hurling grenades and Bren gun fire against two enemy gun emplacements, killing the Germans at the cost of his own life. His bravery was recognized by the Victoria Cross.

Two weeks later at Djebel Garli, Chelu Ram, Company Havildar-Major of the 6th Rajputana Rifles, was at the front of the same advance. Held up by a blazing machine-gun post, Ram, 38, from the Punjab, dashed forward firing a tommy-gun and killed the enemy. Wounded in the battle, he urged on his men in hand-to-hand fighting with other Germans until he died of wounds. Ram was awarded the Victoria Cross.

The mood of such bravery and sacrifice which won final victory, encouraged others to deeds of enormous heroism. Private Charles Duncan, 35, saw a live grenade fall among his comrades. Without hesitation, he threw himself forward and took the force of the explosion – saving everyone except himself. He was awarded the George Cross.

Montgomery

1943

Eighth Army's victory in North Africa made Bernard Montgomery, 45, Britain's most successful and publicized general of the war. Although his predecessors had laid the foundations for Rommel's defeat, it was Montgomery's cautious, meticulous planning, leaving nothing to chance, which transformed dispirited soldiers into a more trained, professional and blood-lusting army.

Montgomery showed loyalty to the 'Desert Rats' who fought across North Africa in his future campaigns in Italy and Europe. Those soldiers without sand in their boots were often shunned, but even those who were respected found a cold, insensitive commander obsessed with small details and who occasionally acted out of spite.

Cheshire – RAF

More than any other pilot, Leonard Cheshire (*above*), born in 1917, personified the legend of Bomber Command. Calm, unpretentious, brilliant and above all awe inspiringly courageous, Cheshire was regarded as one of the greatest British bomber pilots of the war.

The son of a famous lawyer, Cheshire joined the RAF in 1939 and was flying Whitley bombers over Germany the following year. Although badly hit in a bombing run over Cologne, he coaxed the plane back to Britain, winning a DSO and praise for his courage and ability.

By 1943, after surviving two brilliant tours, he was promoted to Wing Commander of 76 Squadron. 'I loved flying,' wrote Cheshire, '[and] I found the dangers of battle exciting and exhilarating so that war came easily to me.' Cheshire rebuilt 617 Squadron's morale after Guy Gibson's death, showing personal concern for each of his 500 men. He developed low-level flying and pinpoint bombing into a fine art. His unconditional bravery – shared by few in Bomber Command, where the mortality rate was so high – was critical in the 617 Squadron pathfinder operations during 1944. Flying between roof level and 200 feet, he facilitated the comprehensive destruction of armament factories in France and Germany by dropping pinpoint markers on the specific targets for the bombers to hit. His Victoria Cross was awarded for 'most conspicuous bravery'.

At the end of the war, after an astounding 100 missions, Cheshire had also won three DSOs and the DFC. In peacetime, he opened and pioneered homes for the incurably sick.

The Dam Busters

16/17 May 1943

On the night of 16/17 May 1943, Wing Commander Guy Gibson, 25, (*above*) – an admired, brave and skilled bomber pilot – was entrusted with the mission to destroy Germany's industrial heartland in the Ruhr. The target of the new 617 Squadron was the Moehne Dam, which, if destroyed, would release tons of water to – hopefully – flood Germany's factories.

Hedge hopping across enemy territory, Gibson led nine Lancasters with special 'bouncing' bombs, invented by Dr Barnes Wallis, towards the artificial lake while the bomb aimers primed the fuses.

With anti-aircraft shells bursting around his plane, Gibson's bomb dropped and exploded near the dam's wall. The concrete held. Gibson guided in the next bombers, even flying alongside in the run-up, deliberately drawing enemy flak. The second Lancaster was hit; the third Lancaster's bomb dropped but again the dam held; the bomb from the fourth Lancaster hit the concrete wall. Suddenly, vast sprays of water – 'like a giant soda siphon' – could be seen from the air as the dam crumbled and the lake began to cascade down the valley.

Celebrated as an idol and hero after his return to Britain, and awarded the Victoria Cross, Gibson wanted to return to operations and defeat Nazism. On 19 September 1944, glimpsing the dawn of victory, his Mosquito was hit during a raid over Germany and he was killed. His posthumously published memoir, *Enemy Coast ahead*, was bought by hundreds of thousands of admirers. Regrettably, German industry was not seriously affected by the collapse of the Moehne Dam.

U-Boat War

Britain's lifeline across the Atlantic was constantly imperilled by Germany's 1,170 U-boats. Marauding the ocean in menacing wolf-packs, the U-boats destroyed 70 per cent of the 2,000 Allied merchant ships lost in the Atlantic. 'The only thing that ever really frightened me during the war', admitted Churchill, 'was the U-boat peril.'

Surfacing at night and slipping stealthily inside the convoys, for the first years of war the U-boat commanders had fired their deadly torpedoes and crashed back into the depths with limited fear of reprisals. Destroying the U-boats depended on RAF patrols undertaking lonely, dangerous operations.

In August 1943, when the accurate tracking of German submarines faltered, Flying Officer Lloyd Trigg, 29 (*right*), Royal New Zealand Air Force, spotted a surfaced U-boat off the West African coast. The approach for the kill was inevitably dangerous. Trigg slowly swung his aircraft into low attack, the U-boat's guns repeatedly hitting his Hudson as it skimmed towards the conning tower. As his plane veered out of control, Trigg dropped his

bombs, witnessed the explosion on the submarine and crashed into the sea. Minutes later, the U-boat sank. Trigg was awarded the Victoria Cross.

By 1944, the heyday of the murderous U-boats was past. Defeated by improved radar, the convoy system, Ultra interception of German communications and in particular, air patrols, the U-boats had been decimated by increasingly sophisticated depth charges. Yet each U-boat at large still posed a considerable risk, especially as the Allies replenished their supplies for the Normandy invasion.

Flying Officer John Cruikshank's (*left*) bravery saved more Allied merchant ships when on 17 July, the 24-year-old from Aberdeen, flying a Catalina on anti-submarine patrol in the North Atlantic, spotted a U-boat.

Turning into the attack, his plane was hit by a hail of flak shells, killing one crew and injuring two others. Flying metal hit Cruikshank in seventy-two places, yet he continued his attack, dropping his depth charges on to the German boat. Gleeful at the sight of explosions and the sinking craft, he turned for the five and a half hour journey home, occasionally losing consciousness but eventually landing successfully. For his bravery, Cruikshank was awarded the Victoria Cross.

Tirpitz

September 1943

The freezing waters of a Norwegian fjord were the target for Lieutenant Donald Cameron, 22, and Lieutenant Basil Place, 23 (*inset*), of the Royal Navy in September 1943. Moored 1,200 miles from Britain in the safety of Kaa fjord was the 42,000 ton *Tirpitz*, sister battleship of the *Bismarck* and its crew of 2,340.

One year earlier, the *Tirpitz*'s eight 15in guns had ravaged a British convoy in the Arctic. Only its own destruction could remove the dire threat to British supply lines across the Atlantic. Invulnerable to air attack in the natural protection of the fjord, the *Tirpitz* could only be attacked by sea. Accordingly, the sabotage operation was assigned to six midget submarines.

On 11 September, six normal submarines slipped out of Loch Carinbawn in Scotland, towing six submerged midgets. Seven days later, the convoy reached Norway. By then, three midgets had been either lost for ever or returned home. Cameron and Place com-

manded two of the remaining three-man midgets. They navigated under the heavy anti-sub nets, covered by guns and anti-submarine mines, to place explosives on the *Tirpitz*'s hull. Both succeeded in penetrating the harbour only to be spotted by lookouts. Mayhem broke out above water as Cameron and Place desperately manoeuvred their craft beneath the *Tirpitz*.

Cameron dumped his mines, primed to explode, and then surfaced to surrender. Place, having fixed his explosives, bombarded by depth charges, also surrendered. By then, Cameron, under interrogation was threatened with immediate execution if he refused to divulge the location of his mines. Sixty minutes had expired when the *Tirpitz* rose violently in the water, sufficiently damaged to be out of action for months. The battleship was finally destroyed by the RAF in 1944.

Both submariners were awarded the Victoria Cross. Cameron, from Lanarkshire, died in 1961 and was buried at sea; Place, from Little Malvern, Worcestershire, died in 1994, having risen to the rank of Rear-Admiral.

White Rabbit – Yeo-Thomas

On the moonless night of 26 February 1943, 'Tommy' Yeo-Thomas (*left*), a romantic buccaneer Special Operations Executive officer, alias 'White Rabbit', parachuted from a Halifax bomber into a Normandy field. The following day, Yeo-Thomas was walking in Paris, beside SS officers, strained by the assumption of another identity, curbing instinctive habits and aware that, if arrested, he had to either stay silent or die fast.

Established by Churchill to 'set Europe ablaze', the SOE's task was to organize a secret army throughout occupied Europe for that future date when the Allies would invade and liberate the continent. Yeo-Thomas's assignment was not to kill Germans but, by sheer force of personality, to persuade warring political factions among the French resistance to cooperate and create a secure organization to engage in subversion and sabotage.

After returning to London briefly in April, Yeo-Thomas landed back in France just as the resistance was reeling from successive betrayals, tortured confessions and demoralization. Betrayed and constantly hunted by the Gestapo, he continued his work – discussing, organizing and encouraging – travelling across France at great risk of exposure.

On his next return to London, in February 1944, Yeo-Thomas personally briefed Churchill that morale in the resistance would remain dire if SOE failed to drop weapons to the combatants. Three weeks later, having secured Churchill's support, he parachuted back into enemy territory. Shortly afterwards in Paris, he was betrayed by a captured resistant and was arrested by the Gestapo.

Repeatedly beaten, but refusing to divulge anything, Yeo-Thomas attempted twice to escape and was eventually sent to Buchenwald concentration camp. En route, he was ready again to escape but refrained when threatened by betrayal from fellow prisoners. When he arrived at the camp, sixteen of those prisoners were executed – slowly strangled near Buchenwald's crematorium. Repeatedly, Yeo-Thomas attempted to escape and finally fled to liberty.

For his courage and outstanding resilience, Yeo-Thomas was awarded the George Cross, the Military Cross, the Légion d'honneur and the Croix de Guerre.

Diana Rowden – SOE

1943

Crossing the French coast at 400 feet under the night cloud on 16 June 1943, Diana Rowden, 28 (*inset*), an officer of the Special Operations Executive, knew her chances of survival were limited but was unaware that a succession of betrayals during previous weeks had already doomed her secret mission.

Guided by three torches shone by the French reception committee, the black Lysander touched down in a remote field near Angers. Minutes later, she had been whisked away to act as a courier for the secret army.

SOE's employment of women agents – young, brave, efficient fluent French speakers who could move more easily than men through occupied France – was an astute break with tradition. The Germans, it was reasoned, would be less suspicious of women coyly explaining their reasons for travel: either to meet their husbands or care for their families. But the best training in radio communications, explosives, combat and endurance could not protect SOE agents from betrayal.

Warnings of danger were flashed from London to Rowden just in time for her to go into hiding. Later she joined another Maquis network in the Jura mountains. Liaising between London and the local resistance, Rowden helped with sabotage and organizing arms drops – 'a woman without fear,' testified a Maquisard – and awaited a new arrival from London.

Disaster struck unexpectedly. The new SOE network had also been penetrated and the reception committee meeting the agent arriving from Britain were Gestapo officers.

Shortly afterwards, the door of Rowden's farmhouse crashed open and the hapless woman was manacled and taken to Avénue Foch, the notorious Gestapo headquarters in Paris. Not only was she tortured, but the knowledge that just outside the building French men and women were enjoying aperitifs in pavement cafés, oblivious to the pain of the freedom fighters, was as distressing as the double betrayal.

On 12 May 1944, Rowden was transported with six other women SOE agents for 'special treatment' to the Natzweiler concentration camp in Germany. On orders from Berlin, each was given a lethal injection of phenol and pushed into the camp's crematorium ovens. After the war, their executors were tracked down, tried and hanged.

Field Marshal Alexander

Harold Alexander (*below right*) was a soldier called upon to serve his country when repeated crisis threatened to end in catastrophe.

Alexander organized the retreat from Dunkirk, not leaving the beach until every British soldier was evacuated; he arrived in Burma on 5 March 1942 and the following day ordered the retreat which saved that army from extinction; on 8 August 1942 he was posted to Cairo and, with Montgomery, saved the 8th Army from defeat; and in 1943 Alexander reorganized the Allied armies in North Africa to defeat the Germans.

Born into a military family in County Tyrone in 1891, Alexander survived the First World War despite three wounds. 'He was reputed to bear a charmed life,' wrote Churchill, 'and under heavy fire men were glad to follow exactly in his footsteps.'

Unruffled under fire and charming to everyone – he was said to defeat his enemies without making any – Alexander's notable qualities were reason, leadership and the ruthless drive to dominate a battlefield. Witnessing his personal courage and concern for his soldiers, they in turn were willing to commit themselves for the ultimate sacrifice. Alexander was 'the ace card in the British Empire's hand,' testified General Eisenhower.

Yet in the 1943-5 Italian campaign, which began with landings on 10 July and welded together an army of many nationalities, even Alexander's qualities were insufficient to win a fast victory. The 1,140 mile trek through mountainous country resulted 530,000 casualties and the blame for such a high cost is partly placed on Alexander's lack of mobility and original, daring tactics.

Promoted to Field Marshal in 1944, Alexander was made a viscount in 1946 and was created Earl Alexander of Tunis in 1952. He died in 1969.

Anzio

February 1944

To break the deadlock of winter in the Italian campaign, 36,000 British and American troops landed on the beaches of Anzio on 22 January 1944. 'Operation Shingle' completely surprised the Germans. Before the Allies lay the road to Rome, 50 miles to the north. But, fatally, the American commander refused to move inland. 'I had hoped that we were hurling a wild cat on to the shore,' wrote Churchill, 'but all we got was a stranded whale.'

Quickly, the Germans counter-attacked and the British were entrapped by a cruel bombardment. By the end of the month, 2,100 had been wounded or killed.

The bitter fighting, joined by 500,000 Germans continued. On 7-8 February, Major William Sidney (later Viscount de l'Isle) (*left*), 5th Battalion, Grenadier Guards, led successive audacious attacks against the Germans, shooting at point blank range

and driving the enemy back. Even after being wounded, he encouraged his men to fight. His gallantry, rewarded by the Victoria Cross, was a small contribution to what had become an unusually intense life- or-death struggle.

Nurses Under Fire

Under the constant threat and noise of bombardment from Germans positioned on the hills overlooking the Anzio beach, Sister Sheila Greaves (*above*) worked thirteen hours a day in the British Casualty Station. Adjacent to the ammunition dump, a long tent had been dug into the sand for operations on wounded soldiers. The badly wounded were evacuated by ship at night. But even the clearly marked red cross did not offer protection. On 21 January, the Luftwaffe bombed two hospital ships, forcing the limbless and badly injured to jump into the water. Greaves was awarded the George Medal for saving many of the casualties.

Cassino

May 1944

In the stagnating battle to reach Rome, the Allies were trapped in the ravines and valleys below the fortified mountain town of Monte Cassino, overlooked by a sixth-century Benedictine abbey.

Between January and May 1944, the Allies – American, New Zealand, French, Indian, Polish, British and other troops – helped by massive air bombardment, launched four major attacks to overcome the German defences and break through to Rome. But the repeated assaults up the hills were repulsed by mines, artillery and withering machine-gun fire, which wiped out whole battalions. 'The tenacity of these German paratroops is quite remarkable,' reported General Alexander to Churchill as the Allied casualties rose to 105,000 and the abbey was destroyed.

Only sheer bravery during that final battle in May and the balance of attrition, finally defeated the Germans. Among the many who risked their lives was Captain Richard Wakeford (*above*), 23, of 2/4 Battalion, the Hampshire Regiment. On 13 May, armed with a revolver, he attacked the enemy, killing several and collecting nearly twenty prisoners. The following day, as the pitch intensified, he again led his men along a knife-edge escarpment to establish a critical position.

In those weeks, hundreds of other soldiers performed equally heroic deeds but, unlike Wakeford and his battalion, did not survive to tell their tale. His Victoria Cross represented the bravery of those hundreds, if not thousands, who fought to liberate Rome on 5 June. Wakeford, a solicitor, died in 1972.

Monte Cassino

On 16 May 1944, Fusilier Francis Jefferson (*left*), 23, the Lancashire Fusiliers, a bricklayer, was lying in a ditch on the mountainside of Monte Cassino. German tanks began advancing towards his company under cover of pitilessly accurate artillery. Without orders, Jefferson grabbed an anti-tank gun – which he had never fired before – and ran forward. Standing in front of the first tank, he pressed the trigger, scored a hit and the tank exploded. A second German tank rapidly reversed. For saving his comrades, King George Vl pinned the Victoria Cross ribbon on to Jefferson in hospital.

On his return to his home town of Ulverston, 2,000 people crowded into the square to honour the hero, and the acclaim continued for years in his local pub. In 1982, a burglar stole Jefferson's medal. Nine months later, devastated and depressed, after tearfully telling his mother that he had nothing to live for, Jefferson walked in front of a train and was killed.

General Sir William Slim

Born in 1891, the son of a Birmingham ironmonger, General William Slim (*below*) was a soldier's soldier. Tall, imposing, bulldog jawed, with unflinching courage and an admired mastery of his profession, he took command of the 14th Army in Burma in October 1943 understanding precisely how, with the loyalty of his troops, he could turn ignominious defeat into victory against the Japanese.

Slim's three pronged advance in Arakan using Brigadier Orde Wingate's 'Chindits' – an American-led army of Chinese and a British-commanded Indian army – stymied a Japanese offensive in Imphal – inflicting the biggest defeat the Japanese army had ever suffered – and saved India.

Slim's next stratagem, along a 700 mile front through the jungle and deploying an extraordinary assortment of armies – British, American, West African, Gurkha, Indian, Chinese and Burmese – was to pursue the Japanese. Crossing the defended 4,100 metre wide river Irrawaddy and launching a brilliant deception operation, Slim's army harassed and attacked the Japanese back to Mandalay and Rangoon.

All those who fought in the 'Forgotten Army', (the 14th), revered Slim as a leader. 'General Slim', wrote Churchill, 'fought valiantly, overcame all the obstacles and achieved the seemingly impossible.' But during the war the Prime Minister barely knew Slim and even discounted the worth of any general with such a surname. Slim's recommendations for how a defeated general in the midst of war should behave offer classic guidance to every aspiring leader: 'In a dark hour he will turn in upon himself and question the very foundations of his leadership and his manhood.

'And then he must stop! For, if he is ever to command in battle again, he must shake off these regrets, and stamp on them, as they claw at his will and his self-confidence. He must beat off these attacks he delivers against himself, and cast out the doubts born of failure, forget them, and remember only the lessons to be learnt from defeat – they are more than from victory.'

So admired were Slim's qualities that he was summoned from retirement in 1948 to become Chief of the Imperial Staff and created a viscount.

The Burma-Siam Railway

For the Japanese High Command it was just a 260 mile railway for moving supplies between Thailand and Burma, but for 61,000 Australian, British and Dutch POWs it was akin to a living death – until 12,000 actually died.

In July 1942, the first 3,000 Allied POWs were transported from Singapore to the disease-infested, humid, mountainous jungle to build first a base camp and then the railway. Since their captors considered their workforce expendable, the POWs lived in appalling housing, without sanitation, without replacement clothes, and with barely any food or medicines to combat the rampant illnesses. Within a brief time, healthy young men had rapidly degenerated into diseased skeletons.

Under constant threat from the Japanese guards, the slave labourers worked sixteen hours a day and were beaten mercilessly at whim. 'No work, no food,' exhorted the Japanese, dumping those about to die in the 'Death House'.

Some POW leaders emerged. Lieutenant Colonel Edward 'Weary' Dunlop of the Royal Australian Medical Corps sought to build comradeship among the desperate men. 'A cold-blooded, merciless crime against mankind,' he wrote in his anguished diary.

At least Dunlop survived. In other Japanese camps, POWs suffered not only starvation and murder, but also rape, torture, mutilation (especially of the genitals), vivisection and even cannibalism: eating the liver cut from prisoners was considered medicinal.

Originally, Japanese engineers advised that the railway would be built in six years. The military told them completion should be within eighteen months. Their success was rewarded by Allied bombing which disrupted the track.

Until the present day, the surviving POWs have received neither compensation nor any apology from the Japanese for suffering those war crimes.

Burma – Gurkhas

1944

Moving with natural stealth and skill, the Gurkha battalions had during 1943 established their fearsome courage in the Burmese jungle. Harrying the Japanese, showing a natural instinct for hunting and killing their enemy, especially in close combat, their battle cry *'Ayo Gurkhali'* ['The Gurkhas are upon you'] struck fear even into that ruthless army.

Rifleman Tulbahadur Pun, 21 (*inset*), from Parbat District, had followed a 150 year Nepalese tradition of serving in the British Army to be seconded to the Chindits, the toughest of shock troops. With that élite, Pun penetrated deep behind enemy lines, sabotaging communications, blowing up bridges and killing Japanese.

Although the Chindits' record was controversial, the Gurkhas' strength, patience and bravery was indisputable. By June 1944, Tulbahadur Pun was truly battle-hardened, when, after a harrowing march through the monsoon and without change of clothing, his battalion was ordered to 'strafe, assault, capture and hold Mogaung', a Japanese occupied town. In an attack on the railway bridge, faced with typical Japanese fanaticism, many of Pun's platoon were rapidly killed. Alone, firing his Bren gun, he stormed across thirty yards of open ground up to the Japanese position, killing three enemy. From there he directed accurate fire until the town was taken. Tulbahadur Pun was awarded the Victoria Cross.

Burma

Under General Slim's personal tutelage during his repeated visits to British Army camps, soldiers had learned how to fight in the jungle, blowing the mystique of Japanese invincibility by understanding the enemy's tactics. Their task, urged 'Uncle Bill', was to destroy an evil empire. The 14th Army trusted Slim and when the Japanese struck, he proved masterful. On that basis, his soldiers were prepared to risk their lives.

Lieutenant George Cairns (*left*), a 31 year old Londoner, was positioned on a hilltop at Henu Block, Burma, in March 1944 when the Japanese attacked, part of the massive 'Imphal Offensive' directed to drive the Allies from blocking the Imperial Army's route to India.

True to their image as fearsome warriors, a Japanese officer hacked off Cairns' left arm. In fury, Cairns retaliated. Shooting his attacker dead, he seized the sword and led a counter-attack.

Slashing at the Japanese, killing and wounding several, he eventually collapsed, but he had magnificently

inspired his comrades to drive back the invaders. His valour was recognized by a Victoria Cross.

Unusually, the fetid jungles and plains of Burma were the natural habitat for Major Frank Blaker (*right*) of the Highland Light Infantry, a 24-year-old who had been born in that country. Commanding a company of the 9th Gurkha Rifles, he was fighting the battle which had already saved India from Japanese occupation and was driving the Emperor's armies back into China. Blaker's Gurkha troops, among the backbone of the Allied forces, had contributed to the biggest defeat of the Japanese army's history by stopping the 1944 Imphal Offensive. It was during the long counter offensive that, in July 1944, Blaker led his company against a well protected Japanese position near Taunghi. As Japanese rifle and light machine-gun fire raked the ground in front of his troops, Blaker, leading from the front, ran towards the hidden emplacements. Although wounded, he carried on and, when he fell, continued to urge his men to storm and capture the enemy's positions. He was awarded the Victoria Cross.

The Great Escape

Deep snow lay outside Stalag Luft III, a German POW camp in Sagan, eastern Germany, on 24 March 1944. For the innocent inmates, bored by imprisonment and anxious to continue fighting the war, planning an escape had been a professional pastime. The moonless night was ideal for an adventure which many had previously attempted and which was permitted under the Geneva Convention.

For one year, 600 POWs had been digging 'Harry', an illuminated, air-conditioned tunnel, supported by 3,000 bedboards which fell 28 feet below a trap door in a hut, turned 90 degrees in the soil and ran 360 feet under the perimeter wire. In emergency, the trap door could be closed and a burning-hot camp stove shoved over the top in twenty seconds.

As teams of seventy-five POWs dug, others were forging passes, manufacturing compasses, sewing clothes, planning escape routes, inventing cover stories, accumulating German money and keeping look-out.

After 11pm on that night, the first of 200 POWs began rolling down the tunnel on a trolley for the synchronized escape, while 1,200 others concealed their absence.

At 4.45am, after seventy-nine had escaped, a sentry outside the camp discovered the breakout hole and fired a shot at a fleeing POW. In the ensuing manhunt, seventy-six POWs were arrested in a wide arc from the North Sea to Czechoslovakia and to the French border. Three reached Britain. By then, on Hitler's orders, fifty escapees had been shot and cremated. For thousands of other Allied POWs and servicemen, those escapees were heroes.

The unsung heroes were the RAF investigators who hunted for the seventy-two Germans responsible for those unlawful executions. Of the thirty-eight convicted, thirteen were hanged and the others imprisoned.

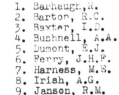
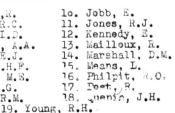

Heimkehrer.

Abtransport am 14.2.44 nach Saarburg.

1. Barhaugh, R.
2. Barton, R.C.
3. Baxter, I.D.
4. Bushnell, A.A.
5. Dumont, E.J.
6. Ferry, J.H.F.
7. Harness, M.E.
8. Irish, A.G.
9. Janson, R.M.
10. Jobb, E.
11. Jones, R.J.
12. Kennedy, E.
13. Mailloux, R.
14. Marshall, D.M.
15. Means, L.
16. Philpit, R.O.
17. Post, R.
18. Quenin, J.H.
19. Young, R.H.

Tedder

In planning the Normandy invasion, Sir Arthur Tedder (*above, third from left*), Eisenhower's deputy from December 1943 to May 1945, orchestrated the huge air attack on German positions to support the Normandy landings. Born in 1890, Tedder was a pilot in the First World War rising to be responsible for aircraft research and development in the years before the outbreak of the Second World War.

In May 1941, posted to the Middle East, Tedder transformed and rebuilt the depleted British Air Force to win air supremacy across the Mediterranean and to develop a new theory, 'Tedder's Carpet', using bombers to clear a path through enemy defences before a ground attack. As a proven mediator with a scientific mind, Tedder advocated combined operations between all three services to secure victory in North Africa.

Anglo-American unity depended upon a good relationship between their army commanders. As America's contribution to the war after the Normandy invasion would be five times greater than Britain's, Tedder's qualities attracted Eisenhower to depend upon the Air Marshal to help plan and execute the war coalition's victory and to mollify Montgomery whose experience in Italy benefited 'Operation Overlord'.

The Nuremberg Raid

30/31 March 1944

The attack on Nuremberg was described as the greatest air battle in history. On 30/31 March 1944 Pilot Officer Cyril Barton (*above*), was flying on a Halifax, one of 795 bombers dispatched to destroy the town which symbolized Adolf Hitler's manic assertions of German dominance and the birth of the 1,000 year Reich. Barton had flown fourteen missions before embarking on this, the latest of Arthur 'Bomber' Harris's blanket bombings.

Seventy miles from the target, after a long flight in dangerously good visibility from a cloudless sky, Barton and the air armada were attacked by German fighters equipped with new radar. Barton's Halifax was damaged and his crew, misunderstanding a signal, bailed out. Alone in the aircraft, Barton continued to his target, dropped his bombs and navigated his 600 mile return to Britain. Crossing the English coast on one engine, his fuel running out and his plane heading towards a village, Barton swung the crippled bomber away from a village and died in the crash landing.

His Halifax was among 94 aircraft lost that night costing over 500 dead or wounded and 159 POWs. The damage to Nuremberg was minimal and the Luftwaffe lost only ten fighters. Barton's sacrifice won him the Victoria Cross, but the horrendous casualties suffered by Bomber Command finally prompted a radical reassessment of strategic bombing.

Preparing the Beaches for the Landings

Long before the first soldier set foot on Normandy's sand, or before any RAF bomber flew across the coast, a small army of engineers and technicians of many skills were dispatched to make the landings possible and safe.

Beaches needed to be cleared of mines, booby traps and obstacles; concrete fortifications were exploded; roads had to be cleared and demolished bridges replaced, often with a Bailey bridge, invented by Sir Donald Bailey. After the first days, a whole harbour was transported and assembled off the French coast and airfields rapidly laid on the beach-head. Preparations began long before June 1944 with the quiet arrival of COPPists like Lieutenant Peter Wild, 28 (*above*), who came ashore in the night to test the incline of the Normandy beaches and the durability of the sand to be certain that tanks and guns could safely disembark and reach land.

On D-Day itself, Wild guided a squadron of Sherman tanks 5,000 yards from the landing craft through rough seas on to the beach. He performed the same task later in Burma. He died in 1995.

Normandy – D-Day

Pegasus Bridge

At sixteen minutes past midnight on 6 June, the first of 153,000 of the Allies' D-Day landing troops gently landed in a glider on a field, fifty yards from the Pegasus Bridge across the river Orne, a vital artery if the D-Day landings later that day were to succeed.

Operation Overlord, the biggest seaborne invasion in history, depended upon meticulous planning, deception of the enemy, air superiority, the destruction of bridges, railways, roads and communications across northern France and, on the day itself, the capture of key installations. And above all – on surprise.

Under the command of Major John Howard 160 men and officers of the 2nd Battalion, the Oxfordshire and Buckinghamshire Light Infantry, were tasked to capture and hold the bridge. Within minutes of the crash landing – knocking most of Howard's soldiers temporarily unconscious – the platoon bundled out of the glider, overwhelmed the scared German defenders and captured the bridge. 'What you get by stealth and guts,' they had been told, 'you must hold with skill and determination'. The reinforcements, members of the Parachute Division, had missed their dropping zone. So under the colossal Royal Navy bombardment from the coast and as the sounds of battle from the beaches intensified, Howard dug in to resist the inevitable German counter-attack.

At 2pm, piercing through the sounds of guns, explosions and automatic fire, Howard caught the music of a Scottish piper. Leading the Commandos of the 1st Special Service Brigade, the piper announced the arrival of Lord Lovat (*inset*), his commander, about to cross the captured bridge. The start of the crusade to liberate Europe was an emotional moment, heralding one small victory and the bitter battle to come.

Violette Szabo

1944

On D-Day+1, Violet Szabo, 23 (*inset*), parachuted into France to join SOE's 14,000-strong army, which had armed 500,000 resistants. Recruited after her husband's death at El Alamein, Szabo's commitment to underground warfare, her patriotism, special hatred of Nazism and zest for adventure had been proven already in an earlier tour along France's Atlantic coast.

In the week before D-Day, thousands of Maquisards had been destroying bridges, railways, telephone lines and canal gates, successfully hampering German reinforcements reaching Normandy. Eisenhower would testify that SOE's networks had been worth six divisions of troops.

Bringing extra weapons for the Maquis, Szabo's task was to help prevent the SS Das Reich Division moving with its tanks north to Normandy. On 8 June, driving armed with a Sten gun along a country road in the Limousin, her driver rashly stopped the car at the sight of German troops. Alerted, the Germans became suspicious, prompting Szabo and her companion to flee. In the rush, Szabo twisted her ankle and, urging the driver to continue, she fired off eight magazines at the advancing SS soldiers before surrendering. After admitting she was English, Szabo was handed over to the Gestapo at their headquarters in Avénue Foch, Paris.

By then, Avénue Foch had become infamous for its torture: scalding baths, cigarette burns, pliers and worse were used to extract information about the identities of resistance networks and their plans. For eight weeks Szabo remained silent. Condemned as a worthless mouth, she was dispatched to Ravensbrück concentration camp.

At seven one evening in early 1945, Szabo, emaciated and dirty, was taken to a yard adjacent to the crematorium and shot through the head by a small calibre pistol. Her corpse was then thrown into the nearby oven. Szabo was one of thirteen SOE women executed.

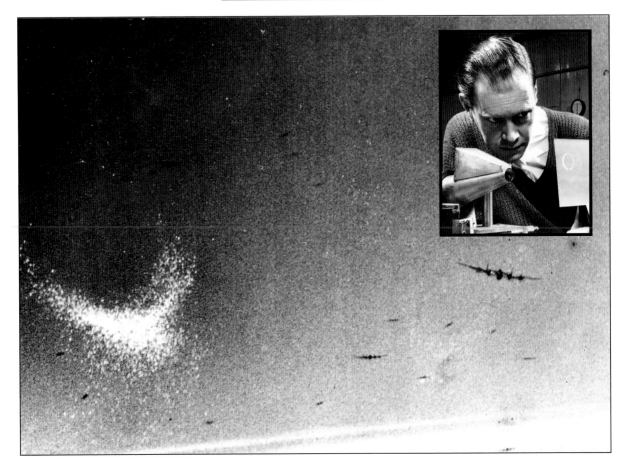

R.V. Jones

Electronic War

The improvement of Bomber Command's performance owed much to the electronic war which started in autumn 1940 when Reginald Jones, 28 (*inset*), the first scientist recruited as an intelligence officer, was called to 10 Downing Street. Churchill and the RAF chiefs wanted an explanation for the deadly accuracy of Germany's bombers during the Blitz.

In hushed tones, Jones described his discovery that the Luftwaffe was using a revolutionary system of intersecting radar beams transmitted from Europe, guiding the bombers directly over their target regardless of the weather. Jones's revelations launched a new war: the battle of the beams. Scientific intelligence, Churchill acknowledged, was essential to close the gap with Germany and win the war.

Like a detective, Jones hunted for evidence about German radar developments and proposed countermeasures to jam the enemy's beams. Simultaneously, new beams were invented to help British bombers find their target in Germany; other beams to confuse German fighters searching for RAF bombers; and new radar for precision bombing.

As the Germans retaliated, Jones proposed in 1943 that RAF bombers scatter tinfoil to confuse enemy radar directing anti-aircraft guns. Again the Germans redressed the balance with airborne radar, shooting down ninety-four RAF bombers on one night in March 1944. D-Day was the climax of the electronic war. Bombarding the Germans along the Channel with a barrage of jamming radar and tinfoil, the chaos bought many valuable hours for the Normandy landings.

After the war, Jones returned to Aberdeen University but remained associated with British intelligence.

Inferno on the Beach

Under the deafening sound of naval gunfire, screeching aircraft and sporadic rifle fire, Sergeant Major Stan Hollis, 32 (*above left*), 6th Battalion, the Green Howards, was carried in that vast armada of over 6,500 ships through the Channel swell. Ahead lay France, clouds of smoke rising from blasted targets and the Normandy beach of La Rivière.

By the time Hollis's feet plunged into the sea, the bodies of earlier arrivals were slumped in the water and sand amid burned-out landing craft. After crawling a few hundred yards inland, rapid fire from a

German machine-gun found and hit Hollis's men. Only sheer courage could silence the threat and Hollis accepted the challenge.

Charging thirty yards to the pillbox with his Sten gun blazing, he inserted the barrel into the slit, sprayed the interior and for good measure thrust inside a grenade. Moving on to the next pillbox, Hollis was gratified to receive the inhabitants' surrender. Twenty-six Germans captured by Hollis alone! Throughout that day, Hollis continued leading his company's charge as if willing himself to win the war singlehanded. His Victoria Cross was the only one awarded on D-Day. Hollis survived the war and returned to Yorkshire to manage a pub.

Churchill in Normandy

In brilliant sunshine on 12 June 1944, Winston Churchill briefly visited Normandy. He was greeted by Montgomery, 'smiling and confident' as the Prime Minister noted, who explained the position at the front three miles away. Churchill inspected the narrow bridgehead, greeted the troops, watched 'a raid by Hun bombers on the harbour' and then returned to his destroyer. 'Why', he asked, 'shouldn't we have a plug at them ourselves before we go home?' After the bombardment, Churchill remarked, 'I admired the Admiral's sporting spirit.'

At dinner that night in Downing Street, Churchill was told that the first flying bombs had hit London, killing civilians. Londoners, he declared excitedly, should be told that their 'tribulations were part of the battle in France, and that they should be very glad to share in the soldiers' dangers.'

Struggling towards Falaise

Few British soldiers slogged further through the Normandy mud against stiff German resistance than 23-year-old Corporal Sidney Bates of the 1st Battalion, Royal Norfolk Regiment. On D-Day Bates had landed at Arramanches with 185th Brigade and marched towards Caen. The swift capture of the town, vital to Allied plans, was delayed first by the absence of tanks and then, contrary to expectations, by fierce enemy retaliation. Strafed by German machine-guns from a defence position dubbed 'Hillman', the Norfolks suffered 150 casualties, wounded or killed, before passing on. For the next month, Bates crouched outside Caen – the victim, according to historians, of bad weather, inferior equipment, poor planning, unadventurous leadership and an absence of bravery among British troops.

By 10 July, the RAF had destroyed Caen and Bates was struggling southwards through the *bocage* – narrow lanes bordered by high banks and hedges surrounded by wooded hills – towards Falaise. Eight hundred thousand Allied troops were in Normandy,

facing stubborn German resistance and counter-attacks.

During one of those German attacks, on 6 August, near Sourdeval, Bates was unexpectedly engaged in close combat. Seizing a light machine-gun, despite a hail of enemy fire, he charged towards the German soldiers. Wounded twice, he continued forwards, shooting at amazed and then fearful Germans. Gradually they retreated, but a third bullet hit Bates. By the time he died two days later, the Allies were again moving forwards. Bates, a Londoner, was awarded the Victoria Cross.

The following day, Captain David Jamieson (*inset*), of the same Royal Norfolk Regiment was battling to defend the bridgehead across the river Orne. The Germans attacked repeatedly over thirty-six hours but Jamieson, wounded and in desperate close combat, fought coolly and determinedly to steady his men until the enemy were finally driven off. His courage and leadership were recognized by a Victoria Cross.

Slaughter in Normandy

On 16 August, thirty survivors of 1/5 Battalion, the Welsh Regiment, were moving south through booby-trapped, hedge-lined cornfields towards the Falaise Gap for the breakthrough to Paris. In recent days, German mortars and shellfire had decimated the battalion's ranks. Upturned rifles plunged into the earth to mark the dead appeared in many fields. On that day, individual courage rather than sheer weight of numbers determined the momentum of advance.

Lieutenant Tasker Watkins, 26 (*inset above*), the battalion's only surviving officer, was groping through the dense countryside. In front was an unbroken line of German infantry supported by panzers. Realizing that only bravery could clinch a breakthrough, Watkins led a bayonet charge, killing fifty Germans. Scattering the survivors of his battalion for the night, Watkins manoeuvred himself to kill the Germans manning a machine-gun post. The following day, the enemy began their retreat towards Falaise and the Allies began their slaughter. 'It was one of the greatest killing grounds of any of the war areas' as Eisenhauer was later to write in his *Crusade in Europe*. 'It was literally possible to walk for hundreds of yards at a time, stepping on nothing but dead and decaying flesh'.

Watkins, awarded the Victoria Cross, became a noted High Court and Appeal Court judge.

Flying in Normandy

After the destruction of Caen, the use of bombers against entrenched German defences became popular to break German strangleholds – not least because bombs saved Allied lives. Although the RAF commanded virtual air superiority over Normandy, the bombers tasked to low flying for pinpoint raids during daylight were occasionally exposed to murderous German ground fire.

Among the thousands of sorties flown in those weeks, Squadron Leader Ian Bazalgette (*right*), a Canadian officer in the RAF's Volunteer Reserve, led a formation of Lancaster bombers towards a tar-

get at Trossy St-Maxim. Skimming over the hedges and ditches, the natural defences which had repeatedly frustrated the Allied advance, Bazalgette's Lancaster was hit, destroying both starboard engines. With fires raging, the 25-year-old from Alberta nevertheless pressed on, accurately bombing his target and turning homewards. He ordered his crew to bail out and landed his crippled plane on the French runway.

Unfortunately, it exploded before he could escape. He and two wounded crewmen were killed. He was awarded the Victoria Cross.

Arnhem

September 1944

By the time Lance Sergeant John Baskeyfield, 21 (*left*), of the South Staffordshire Regiment, was in the midst of the Battle of Arnhem on 20 September, 'Operation Market Garden', General Montgomery's planned masterstroke, was floundering into its third day.

Attached to the 1st Airborne Division, Baskeyfield was among 16,500 paratroops and 3,500 soldiers in gliders who had been committed to reach the Dutch town of Arnhem, establish a bridgehead across the Rhine into Germany and end the war by Christmas.

In charge of a six-pounder anti-tank gun, Baskeyfield was at the front line, painfully discovering the cost of Montgomery's failure to read intelligence reports that two refitted SS panzer divisions were located in the area of the operation. German resistance, helped by bad weather, had stiffened against the slow Allied advances.

According to Montgomery's timetable, the operation should have been completed as Baskeyfield encountered a group of recently refitted Tiger tanks whose crews had just been trained to repel an airborne invasion.

In adversity, Baskeyfield flourished. First, he fired his six-pounder at the awesome Tigers, destroying two; then he fired at a German self-propelled gun. He missed and his own gun was hit by enemy fire, wounding him and his crew. Bleeding, he crawled to another abandoned gun and singlehandedly fired twice, hitting the German gun before he was killed. Baskeyfield was awarded the Victoria Cross.

Retreat from Arnhem

Blame for the defeat at Arnhem could not be placed upon those field officers whose dedication and courage would have brought victory if their generals had performed properly.

One such officer was Major Robert Cain, 35 (*below left*), of the Royal Northumberland Fusiliers, who, because of the failure of his superiors' planning and execution, found himself cut off from his battalion. Surrounded by German tanks, self-propelled guns and infantry, he moved ceaselessly among his troops, encouraging them to continue fighting. Disregarding his wounds, Cain eventually managed to lead the survivors to safety. He was awarded the Victoria Cross and settled in Nigeria after the war, working for Shell.

There was also the sacrifice of Captain Lionel Queripel, 24 (*below right*), 10th Parachute Battalion, from Monkton, Dorset. Although wounded, he refused the order to retreat and, armed with a pistol and grenades, insisted on covering his men's withdrawal. He was never seen again. Queripel was awarded the Victoria Cross.

Two days later, Montgomery ordered the retreat, abandoning about 1,600 dead and 6,000 who had been captured. In the aftermath, Montgomery criticized the American army and argued with Eisenhower for refusing to support a single push towards Berlin. His conceited manner irritated those who might otherwise have praised him.

Holland – Stretcher Bearers

February 1945

For front-line combat soldiers, especially Commandos, it was reassuring to know that in the event of injury the stretcher-bearers of the Royal Army Medical Corps were not far behind. Paramedics like Lance Corporal Henry Harden, 33 (*inset*), from Northfleet, Kent, attached to 45 Royal Marine Commando in Holland in early 1945, were in the midst of the advance into Germany. They heard the cries of the wounded and the dying: 'Mother, I love you,' the final words of so many brave young men.

Battlefield medicine had improved enormously since the First World War. Better drugs and blood plasma gave casualties in 1945 twenty-five times the chance of full recovery. Unlike his predecessors,

Harden was mobile and knew that behind him was an efficient conveyor belt of qualified and well-equipped doctors to treat the wounded.

So in the midst of an attack on 23 January 1945, Harden rushed across 100 yards of open ground under fire to assist three wounded marines. Two were brought back, but on the third journey Harden was shot dead. He was awarded the Victoria Cross and was buried in Holland.

Into the Reich

25 February 1945

Flushing out buildings inhabited by the unseen enemy in close combat was a perilous undertaking, but vital to secure the advance of a whole army. Without individual acts of fearless bravery to challenge the entrenched enemy, the advance through Holland into Germany in February 1945 would have ground to a halt.

A mixture of fury and bravery motivated 19-year-old Royal Scots Fusilier Dennis Donnini (*inset*) to storm an occupied house near the river Maas, throw a grenade through a window and pursue the fleeing enemy with his Bren gun firing until he was killed.

Donnini's example inspired his comrades and hastened the invasion of Nazi Germany, as did Sergeant Aubery Cosen's act of bravery.

On the night of 25/26 February, Cosen, 24, from Ontario, Canada and a member of the Canadian Queen's Own Rifles was leading the remnants of his platoon at Mooshof near Wesel on the Dutch-German border, in the north flank assault to clear the Germans from west of the Rhine. Directing his men to give him covering fire, he ran towards an Allied tank, directing its fire from outside. Then, edging forward, directing the tank to crash into a building, he killed several defendants and took the remainder prisoner. Undaunted, he repeated the operation on two more buildings before falling, the victim of a sniper. He won the Victoria Cross.

Italy

Autumn 1944

By autumn 1944, Private Henry Burton, 21 (*right*), of the Duke of Wellington's Regiment, and Captain John Brunt, 22 (*far right*), of the Sherwood Foresters, had spent more than a year fighting up the Italian peninsula. Contrary to the original plan, which envisaged the rapid capture of the country, it had been an horrendous grind. Hampered by rain, mountains and German resistance,

every inch of territory gained had cost lives. After a year, Burton and Brunt, part of the 8th Army, were bogged down in tough terrain by glutinous mud. While for some American generals Italy had become an expensive sideshow, General Alexander was determined to lead the 8th Army into Vienna and ordered an advance up the Adriatic coast. The Germans had other ideas.

British success depended upon individual acts of bravery. Burton, born in Melton Mowbray, Leicestershire, displayed that exceptional courage on 8 October at Monte Ceco. Rushing forward firing his tommy-gun, he

killed Germans manning a Spandau and two machine-guns and then resisted a counter-attack before being killed. His total disregard for his own safety, during many hours of fierce fighting in mud and continuous rain, was an inspiration to all his comrades.

Two months later, on 9 December, Brunt's platoon had dug in around a house near Faenza, west of Rimini, facing fierce German opposition. Suddenly, heavy and accurate German mortar fire destroyed the house. Abandoning the wounded, Brunt rallied the outnumbered survivors to face the enemy's advance.

In front of his men, Brunt seized a Bren gun and personally killed at least fourteen Germans. Having used all his ammunition, he began firing heavier guns, including a mortar. The enemy retreated and Brunt ran back to the destroyed house to organize help for the wounded. Throughout the remainder of that day, the captain from Chirbury, Shropshire, continued to lead the counter-attack until he was killed.

In recognition of their bravery, both Brunt and Burton were awarded the Victoria Cross.

The advance up Italy remained practically paralysed.

Behind the Lines

Using guile and common sense, RAF officers brought down behind enemy lines always tried to escape imprisonment and return to Allied lines. Conditions in Italy made their escapes easier than from Germany: many Italians were friendly; Allied armies were fighting in Italy; and there were helpful British and Irish nationals in the Vatican City. But Sergeant Arthur Banks, 21, 112 Squadron, Desert Air Force, RAFVR, from Wales, was among the unfortunate.

Flying a reconnaissance mission in the Ravenna area on 27 August 1944, Banks's aircraft was hit and forced to land in Rovigo. During his attempt to move south towards the Allied lines, he met local partisans and joined their fight against the Germans. In December, attempting to cross the Po to return to the Allies, the group was captured. The Germans handed Banks to Italian fascist officers. For weeks he was brutally tortured – his stomach and genitals were burned with hot irons, and there was worse – for information. Miraculously, Banks grabbed a machine-gun but was betrayed by his fellow captives. He was tortured again, stripped, bound and thrown into the Po. Half dead, he crawled on to the bank and was shot in the head.

Two Italians were subsequently executed for his murder and several accomplices, including a woman, were imprisoned. Banks was awarded the George Cross.

Italy – Operation Grapeshot

April 1945

To have fallen with the end of the war in sight is bitter-sweet, yet only those last sacrifices could demolish German military power in Italy for ever.

British Commandos and special forces spear-headed the final breakthrough on 2 April 1945. In 'Operation Grapeshot', the ferocity of their attack was designed to deceive the Germans that Lake Comacchio, near Ravenna, was the location and centre of the Allied advance.

Major Anders Lassen (*top*), 25, Special Boat Service, No. 1 SAS Regiment, from Denmark, and Corporal Thomas Hunter (*bottom*), 22, 43rd Royal Marine Commando, from Aldershot, were part of the special forces' assault on the German position.

Success could only be won with daring and mobility. Grabbing a Bren gun, Hunter charged across 200 yards of open ground towards a German nest of three machine-guns, drawing fire while the remainder of his troop took a safer route. When he reached the position, six Germans surrendered and the remainder fled. Reloading, Hunter continued his charge and was killed, firing accurately to the last. The position was won.

Six days later, in a similar operation, Lassen was detailed to 'shoot up' the enemy. Dozens of Germans were killed before he was wounded, but he refused to be evacuated until the operation was completed. He died of his wounds.

Deceived by those attacks, the German army was thrown off balance. The full force of the British 8th Army and Fifth US Army struck in the Argenta Gap, breaking the back of German resistance near Bologna and galloping for final victory towards Genoa, Milan and Venice.

The sacrifice of Hunter and Lassen contributed to forcing the German surrender on 2 May. Both were awarded the Victoria Cross and were buried in the Argenta Gap. The 8th Army had suffered 123,254 casualties in the Italian campaign. The Fifth US Army had suffered 188,746.

The Battle for Germany

1 March 1945

In January 1945 – despite the intense bombardment of Germany by the RAF and US air force, the Royal Navy's blockade and invasion on two fronts – the resistance met by British troops crossing on to German soil was unceasingly ferocious.

More than ever, as fanatical defenders fought to save their Fatherland, each British soldier required extra courage to engage in the close combat necessary to flush out the enemy, deliver a mortal blow to the last gesture of defiance, pass over the corpses and roll on to the next pocket of resistance.

Victory depended upon anonymous squaddies like Private Jim Stokes, 30, the King's Shropshire Light Infantry, from Lanark. On 1 March 1945, Stokes was pinned down by intense rifle and machine-gun fire coming from a farm building near Krevenheim. In a moment of bravery, firing from the hip, he rushed the building and captured the entire twelve-man gun crew. On another building, he performed the same feat and captured five. On the third attempt, wounded but refusing medical aid, he finally fell just before the objective was taken.

On the same day, sixty miles south, Major Frederick Tilston (*inset*), Canadian Infantry Corps from Toronto, led the charge through the Hochwald Forest, taking two machine-gun posts and, when wounded, successfully encouraging his men to push forwards and hold the new position. Both Stokes and Tilston received the Victoria Cross. Montgomery moved forward to prepare for the crossing of the Rhine.

The Bombardment of Germany

1 April 1945

Standing on a hill overlooking the Rhine in the early hours of 24 March 1945, after a bombardment by 2,000 guns and 3,000 planes and the dispatch of 14,000 airborne troops behind enemy lines, Churchill watched the British Army cross the wide waterway. As RAF fighters spewed flames and German shells exploded, he lamented that 'Imagination built on a good deal of experience told a hard and painful tale.'

The heroes at the climax were in the front line, firing from the hip, leading the charge. Among them was Corporal Edward Chapman (*inset below*), 25, 3rd Battalion, the Monmouthshire Regiment, from Glamorgan, Wales. On 1 April, pinned down near the Dortmund-Ems Canal and surrounded by casualties, Chapman charged the enemy firing his Bren at point-blank range, and began carrying his wounded company commander to the rear for help, firing over his other shoulder. Unfortunately, his commander was killed and Chapman himself

wounded, but his gallantry was recognized with the Victoria Cross.

Eighty miles north, near Lingen, Captain Ian Liddell, 26 (*inset above*), 5th Battalion Coldstream Guards, noticed that 500lb bombs had been attached to a key bridge across the river Ems. Commanded to take the bridge, Liddell ran forward alone, scaled a ten-foot high road block and, under intense enemy fire disconnected the wires to the bombs. His work completed, he climbed back over the road block and ordered his platoon's advance. Liddell did not personally receive his Victoria Cross. Eighteen days later he was killed in action.

The Fall of Germany

21 April 1945

On 21 April, as Soviet soldiers in Berlin fought street by street towards Hitler's bunker, Guardsman Edward Charlton, 24, of the Irish Guards, was in the midst of a bitter battle against more fanatical German defenders in Wistedt, between Bremen and Hamburg. Charlton was among over five million Allied troops fighting in western Europe. Since the Normandy landings 200,000 had been killed by stubborn German defenders.

In that ferocity, Charlton's troop of tanks with supporting infantry were barely aware of Germany's imminent surrender. Having captured the village, the Guards were suddenly stormed in a fierce counter-attack. Without warning, Charlton seized a Browning and advanced, firing from the hip. His sheer audacity stunned the Germans, inflicting heavy casualties. The enemy advance was halted, but Charlton, although wounded, placed his gun on a fence and maintained rapid fire, saving the lives of several comrades, until he was captured. He died later that day, remembered by his troop for his inspiring gallantry, for which he won the Victoria Cross.

Burma

In the Burmese jungle, Slim had proved himself a brilliant defensive general and then an outstanding tactician. In an astonishingly bold move around the river Irrawaddy, he moved a whole Army corps down a bullock-cart track to outflank the waiting Japanese army. Slashing through the jungle, the enemy was caught by surprise.

In that hazardous operation, leading to the monumental attack to recapture Rangoon, Naik Gian Singh (*above*), 25, Indian Army, firing his tommy-gun, rushed the Japanese foxholes, hurling grenades covered in blood from his wounds, killing a swath of enemy and contributing to the historic victory. His Victoria Cross was gazetted just before the Japanese fled Rangoon and the liberation of Burma was assured.

New Guinea

March 1945

Australia's front-line defence against the Japanese was fought in the inhuman and unimaginable disease-ridden island of New Guinea, north of Australia. Sergeant Tom Derrick, 30, from Murray River and Lieutenant Albert Chowne (*inset*), 25, from Sydney, were two of the Australian brigade who suffered terrible conditions to drive the Japanese from the island.

Since March 1942, most Australian casualties had been caused by malaria, typhus, dysentery or soldiers falling into quicksand, plunging into gorges or mistakenly slipping into the jungle, never to be seen again. Exhausted by merely chopping a few feet of rainforest vegetation, Derrick and Chowne's jungle-rotting, hungry comrades had called themselves 'swamp rats' for surviving poisonous insects and blood-sucking leeches. At least the Australians, unlike the Japanese, did not resort to cannibalism.

On 24 November 1943, Derrick's platoon stormed Japanese positions outside Sattelberg. Driven back by intense fire, Derrick volunteered to go forward alone. Throwing grenades, he demoralised the Japanese into fleeing the township.

In March 1945, the three-year campaign masterminded by the American General Douglas McArthur was nearing victory. Chowne's platoon was engaged in the final onslaught through the treacherous Torricelli mountains towards the Japanese headquarters in Wewak. Ahead, a platoon was taking heavy casualties from an entrenched Japanese position, when Chowne committed himself to an act of courageous anger against an inhuman enemy. Rushing forward, he threw grenades at two startled Japanese machine-gunners, killing both and, with machine-gun blazing, charged the position. Within fifty yards he fell, mortally wounded. Six weeks later Wewak fell.

Both Chowne and Derrick were awarded the Victoria Cross. Derrick died in Borneo in May 1945.

Midget Submarine in Japan – Takao

31 July 1945

After a thirteen-hour, hazardous, submerged journey in the midget submarine XE.3 in the Jahore Straits, Singapore, Lieutenant Ian Fraser (*left*), 25, from London, and Able Seaman Jim Magennis (*right*), 26, from Belfast, parked their craft underneath the hull of the Japanese cruiser *Takao*. Considering the human suffering caused by the Imperial Army and Navy, their task, to attach limpet mines to the cruiser, would be welcome revenge.

After squeezing through the partly opened diving hatch, Magennis swam towards the hull, endangered by leaking breathing apparatus. He methodically scraped off barnacles, attached the mines and, exhausted, squeezed back into the submarine.

As Fraser began their return journey, he discovered the submarine was immobile. Aware that just above him was the merciless enemy, he ordered Magennis to return to the water despite limpet mines ticking towards detonation. For over five nerve-wracking minutes, Magennis released carriers attached to the craft and then re-entered the midget. Still unseen, the midget navigated its return to safety, mission accomplished. The mines exploded and the cruiser was damaged. Both men were awarded the Victoria Cross.

Victory

At 3pm on 7 May, from the Cabinet Room at 10 Downing Street, Churchill broadcast to the nation announcing the surrender of Germany and the ending of hostilities 'one minute after midnight tonight'.

In five years, 264,443 British servicemen had been killed, 40,000 had gone missing, and 277,077 had been wounded. In Britain, 60,595 civilians had been killed.

The whole nation listened to Churchill recall how for one year Britain had fought the war alone, until 'Finally almost the whole world was combined against the evil-doers, who are now prostrate before us.' With his voice breaking, Churchill ended, 'Advance Britannia! Long live the cause of freedom! God save the King.'

As he left the Cabinet Room, he was greeted by cheering and clapping staff lining the corridors. On the drive from Downing Street to Parliament Square, huge crowds brought Churchill's car to a halt. Inside the House of Commons, every member stood and yelled and yelled with glee. Emotions engulfed and united the members. Despite the war, democracy had survived. Without Churchill, the war might have been lost.

Once more in Parliament Square, Churchill told the vast, joyous crowd, 'This is not a victory of a party or of any class. It's a victory of the great British nation as a whole.' His message to future heroes was moving: 'Do not despair, do not yield to violence or tyranny, march straight forward and die if need be – unconquered!'

Picture Credits p1 Corporal Leslie Allan of Ballarat Vic carrying an American to safety, Mt Tambu, New Guinea (ETA) p2/3 Canadian troops going ashore from a Landing Craft Infantry, Normandy, June 1944 (RH) p9 Lieutenant-Commander Gerard Broadmead Roope (IWM) p9 HMS *Glowworm* survivors, April 1940 (IWM/ETA) p10 Captain Bernard Armitage Warburton-Lee (IWM) p10/1 Results of Blitzkrieg, France, 1940 (B/ETA) p11 German plane bombs French tank in the Blitzkrieg, 1940 (B/ETA) p12/3 Coventry after the night blitz, 16 November 1940 (HD) p13 Prime Minister Winston Churchill surveying ruins (RH) p14 Lieutenant Christopher Furness (IWM) p14/5 German troops, Arras, France, May 1940 (B/ETA) p15 German infantry, Aisne, France, 1940 (IWM/ETA) p16 Dunkirk, May 1940 (IWM/ETA) p17 Captain Harold Andrews (IWM) p17 Royal Tank Regiment evacuation from Dunkirk, May 1940 (IWM/ETA) p18 Able Leading Seaman Jack Mantle (TE) p18 The gun crew of a minesweeper (TRH) p19 Air Vice-Marshal Keith Park (IWM) p19 WAAF fighter plotters in the Hole at Bentley Priory, Fighter Command (IWM/ETA) p20 Flight Lieutenant Eric James Brindley Nicolson (IWM) p20/1 Men and Hurricanes of 87 Squadron, France, March 1940 (IWM/ETA) p22 Wing Commander Brendan 'Paddy' Finucane (IWM) p22 Reginald J. Mitchell (CBC) p22/3 Factory floor (Vickers Ltd) p24 Captain Michael Blaney (TE) p24/5 Air raid damage in the City (from the Dome of St. Paul's Cathedral), 29 December 1940 (RH) p25 Bank of England and Royal Exchange, crater was Bank Underground Station, 11 January 1941 (RH) p26/7 Douglas Bader and Canadian pilots of his squadron 242 (IWM/ETA) p27 Hurricanes (TRH Pictures) p28 Captain Edward Stephen Fogarty Fegen (IWM) p28/9 The Battle of the Atlantic (IWM) p30 Bridging the river Ems, 1 April 1945 (IWM) p30 The Dortmund-Ems Canal (CBC) p31 Lancasters of XV Squadron setting out for Germany (CBC) p31 Flight Lieutenant Roderick Alastair Brook Learoyd (IWM) p31 Flight Sergeant George Thompson (IWM) p32 General Archibald Wavell (IWM) p32/3 Tobruk with fires burning after capture by British and Australian forces, 24 January 1941 (IWM/ETA) p34 German General Guderiano in command vehicle in France, June 1940 with his Enigma machine (IWM/ETA) p35 Bletchley Park (ETA) p35 Alan Turing (ETA) p36 Italian Alpine troops during Wavell's Offensive, Bengasi, North Africa (RH) p36 Corporal John Hurst Edmondson (IWM) p37 Sergeant John Daniel Hinton (IWM) p37 Metaxa line, Crete (RH) p38 General Student and members of a parachute unit, Invasion of Crete (P) p38/9 German Alpine troops crossing a brook during their advance in Crete (P) p39 Lieutenant Charles Hazlitt Upham (IWM) p40 Brest dockyard showing *Scharnhorst* and *Gneisenau* (IWM) p40 Flying Officer Kenneth Campbell (IWM) p41 *Bismarck* engaging HMS *Hood* which was blown up 24 May 1941. Photograph taken from the *Prinz Eugen* (IWM/ETA) p42 British shells bursting near Hell Fire Pass (Hlafaya Pass) in North Africa, 20 May 1941 (IWM/ETA) p42 Lieutenant Colonel Geoffrey Charles Tasker Keyes (IWM) p43 Sidi Rezegh, November 1941 (RH) p43 Brigadier John (Jock) Charles Campbell (IWM) p44 Captain Philip John Gardner (IWM) p44 Captain James Joseph Bernard Jackman (IWM) p44 Another bomb exploding in front of one of our tanks (IWM/ETA) p45 Churchill (IWM) p45 Pearl Harbor, 7 December 1941 (ETA) p46 Heavy bombing in Malta, 13 April 1942 (RH) p46 Inhabitants salvaging belongings from a bomb-wrecked building in Valetta, Malta (RH) p47 General Sir Hastings Ismay (IWM) p47 Churchill's bedroom in Fortress Whitehall (RH) p48 Lieutenant Colonel Arthur Edward Cumming (IWM) p48 Japanese lorries crossing an improvised bridge over the Causeway linking Johore Baru with Singapore (HD) p48/9 English open anti-aircraft barrage in Singapore (RH) p50 Japanese landing parties charge into Hong Kong (RH) p51 (left) Corporal James Clark Gordon (left) and Gunner Norman Hill when liberated by US Pacific Fleet from Formosa Prison Camp, Japan (HD) p51 (right) Aomori, Japanese internment camp near Yokohama two Allied POWs after being freed by US Navy forces, 28 August 1945 (RH) p52 Admiral Sir Max Horton (IWM/ETA) p52 Admiral Sir Max Horton in operations room (IWM/ETA) p53 Vera Lynn in Trafalgar Square, 10 June 1943 (HD) p54 Lieutenant Commander Eugene Kingsmill Esmonde (IWM) p54 *Prinz Eugen* in the English Channel (RH) p54/5 German squadron in English Channel (RH) p56 HMS *Campbeltown* in St Nazaire just before she blew up together with the dry dock (RH) p57 The British dead in St Nazaire (RH) p57 British Naval personnel captured in St Nazaire (RH) p57 Lieutenant Commander Stephen Halden Beattie (IWM) p57 Commander 'Red' Robert Edward Dudley Ryder (IWM) p57 Able Seaman William Alfred Savage (IWM) p58 Air Vice-Marshal Sir Charles Portal inspecting members of a Spitfire Squadron (RH) p59 Dr Archibald McIndoe with the Guinea Pig Club (Queen Victoria Hospital, East Grinstead) p60/1 Bomb damage in Cologne, Germany (RHPL) p61 Flying Officer Leslie Thomas Manser (CBC) p62/3 Dead and wounded on beach after Dieppe raid, 19 August 1942 (IWM/ETA) p63 Captain Patrick Anthony Porteous (IWM) p64 Admiral Sir Andrew Brown Cunningham, Commander-in-Chief of the Mediterranean fleet, 14 August 1940 (IWM/ETA) p64 Aircraft carrier HMS *Indomitable* and HMS *Eagle* during Pedestal convoy Malta with reconnaissance and torpedo bomber and Sea Hurricanes (ETA) p65 Lieutenant Commander Malcolm David Wanklyn (IWM) p65 HM Submarine *Turbulent* with crew and Commander John Linton (IWM) p66 Petty Officer Thomas William Gould (IWM) p66 The Battle of the Atlantic (IWM/ETA) p66 Lieutenant Peter Scawen Watkinson Roberts (IWM) p67 Private Arthur Stanley Gurney (IWM) p67 Sergeant Keith Elliott (IWM) p67 German tank advancing during fighting, Western Desert, North Africa, June 1942 (IWM/ETA) p68 Axis soldiers crouch under a ridge seeking shelter in the thick of the battle, Western Desert, North Africa, 16 November 1942 (HD) p69 Lieutenant General Montgomery (RH) p69 Sergeant William Henry Kirby (IWM) p70 Wing Commander Hugh Gordon Malcolm (IWM) p70 Armoured car crew watch German fighter downed by British, 8 June 1942 (IWM/ETA) p70 Business as usual outside the 'Control Office' (RH) p71 Colonel David Stirling greeting a SAS ('Desert Rat') jeep patrol on its return from the North African desert (IWM) p72 Maquis in Haute Loire, France (HD) p73 Major General Colin Gubbins (IWM) p73 Odette Samsom showing her George Cross to two of her daughters, Francoise (14) and Lille (12) outside Buckingham Palace, 19 November 1946 (HD) p74 Lieutenant Airey Neave after his attempt to escape dressed as a German, 1941 (IWM) p74/5 Colditz Castle (IWM) p76/7 Still from the film 'The Cockleshell Heroes' (British Film Institute) p77 Captain H.G. 'Blondie' Hasker in bow of canoe MK2 and Royal Marine Commando Stewart in stern (Royal Marines Museum) p78/9 A 4.5inch gun of 64 Medium Regiment Royal Artillery Eighth Army bombards the Mareth Line, North Africa, 27 February 1943 (IWM) p79 Lieutenant Colonel Derek Anthony Seagrim (IWM) p80 Lieutenant Colonel Lorne Campbell (IWM) p80 Captain Lord Charles Anthony Lyell (IWM) p80/1 An infantryman dodging flying rocks and splinters, North Africa (IWM/ETA) p81 Wadi Akarit prisoners, 12 April 1943 (IWM) p82 General Montgomery with two captured German Generals (fixing assembly points for the enemy units), May 1943 (IWM/ETA) p83 Whitley V, ex-78 Squadron (CBC) p83 Wing Commander Geoffrey Leonard Cheshire (IWM) p84 Wing Commander Guy Penrose Gibson (IWM) p84 Air Chief Marshal Sir Arthur 'Bomber' Harris with Dambusters of Mohne Dam (IWM/ETA) p85 Dambusters raid, Mohne Dam, Germany, 17 May 1943 (RH) p86/7 Mosquitos from RAF Coastal Command attack U-Boats, 6 May 1945 (ETA) p87 Flying Officer John Alexander Cruikshank (IWM) p87 Flying Officer Lloyd Allen Trigg (IWM) p88 Lieutenant Basil Charles Godfrey Place (IWM) p88 Lieutenant Donald Cameron (*centre back row*) with Sublieutenant J.T. Lorimer (*right, back row*), Sublieutenant R.H. Kendall (*left, front row*) and R.K..A. Goddard (*2nd from left, front row*), crew of submarine attack on Tirpitz, 1942 (IWM/ETA) p89 *Tirpitz* at Narvik, July 1942 (IWM) p90 Wing Commander Forest 'Tommy' Yeo-Thomas (HD) p91 B-17 Flying fortress of the 8th AAF Skies dropping supplies to Maquis (HD) p93 General the Honourable Sir Harold Alexander (IWM) p94 Major William Sidney (HD) p94/5 Allied landings at Anzio. A German 15cm armoured heavy infantry howitzer in a firing position in the ruins of Carroceto, 26 February 1944 (IWM) p95 Sister Sheila Greaves (IWM) p96 Captain Richard Wakeford (IWM) p96/7 Cassino after victory, May 1944 (IWM/ETA) p97 Infantrymen search a partly-demolished building in Cassino for snipers, 24 March 1944 (RHPL) p98 Fusilier Francis Arthur Jefferson (IWM) p98/9- Battle for the Cassino Plain. Encircling attack by 6th Battalion Inniskillings advancing through smoke screen past Monastery Hill, May 1944 (RH) p100 General William Slim (RH) p101 Nakom Paton Japanese Hospital Camp, Thailand (IWM) p102 Gurkhas cutting bamboo stakes to protect their positions, Imphal, Burma (IWM) p102 Rifleman Tulbahadur Pun (IWM) p103 Chindits crossing river Chindwin, Burma (RH) p105 Major Frank Gerald Blaker (IWM) p104/5 A British mortar team in action at the Battle of Imphal-Kohima, Burma, 1944 (IWM) p105 Lieutenant George Albert Cairns (IWM) p106 POWs who escaped from Stalag Luft III, Sagan, Germany (IWM) p107 Planning invasion: (from left) Lieutenant General Omar N Bradley, Admiral Sir Bertram Ramsay, Air Chief Marshal Sir Arthur Tedder, Allied Supreme Commander Eisenhower, General Sir Bernard Montgomery, Air Chief Marshal Sir Trafford Leigh-Mallory and Lieutenant General Walter Bedell Smith (P) p108 Cyril Joe Barton (CBC) p108 Gladbeck, Germany HP Halifax B.III, MZ759, NP-Q of 158 Squadron hit by flak and on fire, 24 March 1945 (CBC) p109 Halifax bombers over Calais during a daylight attack on fortified German garrison positions, 25 September 1944 (IWM) p111 German guards at Atlantic Wall (RH) p110/1 the lines of communication at the Atlantic Wall (RH) p112 Lieutenant Colonel Lord Lovat (HD) p112 Normandy Landings a low level reconnaissance photograph showing Horsa Gliders and parachutes on the Landing Zones near Ouistreham, 6 June 1944 (IWM) p113 Violette Szabo (HD) p113 Maquis and Free French in Normandy. (RH) p114 Lancaster dropping tin foil to interfere with ground gunners during 1,000 bomber raid on Essen, Germany, 11 March 1945 (IWM/ETA) p114 R.V. Jones (R.V. Jones) p115 Aluminium foil (code-named window) used to interfere with ground gunners (IWM/ETA) p116 Sergeant Major Stanley Elton Hollis (IWM) p116 D-Day troops assembling on beach from landing craft (IWM/ETA) p116/7 D-Day landings on Normandy beaches, 6 June 1944 (IWM/ETA) p118 Churchill with General Montgomery, Normandy, 12 June 1944 (IWM) p119 Captain David Auldgo Jamieson (IWM) p119/120 Sherbrooke Foresters following tank in battle of Falaise Gap, France 1944 (ETA) p120 Lieutenant Tasker Watkins (IWM) p121 -Two Canadian soldiers search out enemy elements left in this village, captured during the advance on Falaise, France, 12 August 1944 (RHPL) p122/3 Halifaxes and Lancasters bomb an ammunition depot north of Falaise, France, 1944 (CBC) p123 Squadron Leader Ian Willoughby Bazalgette (CBC) p124 Lance Sergeant John Daniel Baskeyfield (IWM) p124/5 Dakotas and parachute drop over Arnhem (IWM) p126 Paratroops in Gosserbech, Germany, 23 September 1944 (IWM/ETA) p126 Major Robert Henry Cain (IWM) p126 Captain Lionel Ernest Queripel (IWM) p127 Battle of Arnhem, Holland (RH) p128 Lance Corporal Henry Eric Harden (IWM) p128 Wounded British soldier attended to by stretcher bearers in Nijmegen, Holland, February 1945 (HD) p129 Fusilier Dennis Donnini (IWM) p129 British 2nd Army watch the road near Geljesteren on the banks of the Maas, December 1944 (HD) p130 R.A.M.C. orderlies carry wounded Germans in for treatment, Casaglia, Italy, October 1944 (HD) p131 Captain John Henry Cound Brunt (IWM) p131 Private Richard Henry Burton (IWM) p131 8th Army front Sangrian sector after torrential rain for 4 days, 3 October 1944 (IWM) p132 Lysander plane surrounded by Partisans after landing, 14 April 1945, Cuneo-Alba area (IWM) p133 Major Anders Frederich Emil Victor Lassen (IWM) p133 Maori troops cross Fuimicino River, Italy, 11 October 1944 (IWM) p133 Corporal Thomas Peck Hunter (IWM) p134 the 15th Scottish Division makes a safe landing on the east bank of the Rhine, 24 March (RH) p134/5 As dawn breaks, British troops board the assault boats in which they will cross the Rhine on the 24 March (RH) p135 Major Frederick Tilston (IWM) p136 Corporal Edward Thomas Chapman (IWM) p136 53rd Heavy Regiment R.A. shelling enemy positions and guns across the river Elbe, Germany, 1945 (RH) p137 Captain Ian Oswald Linton Liddell (IWM) p137 British infantry of the 3rd Division in action against German snipers in Lingen, Germany (RH) p138 British troops east of the Rhine move forward along a road littered with German dead (RH) p139 Naik Gian Singh (IWM) p139 Sikh patrol charging a Japanese foxhole, Burma, April 1945 (RH) p140 Lieutenant Albert Chowne (IWM) p140 Australian patrol in Lae, New Guinea, 6 October 1943 (RH) p141 Able Seaman Jim Magennis (HD) p141 Lieutenant Ian Edward Fraser (IWM) p141 *Takao* on her trials, 31 March 1932 (IWM) p142 Churchill in Whitehall, VE Day (P)

Bundesarchiv/E.T. Archive (B/ETA), Chaz Bowyer Collection (CBC), E.T. Archive (ETA), Hulton-Deutsch Collection (HD), Imperial War Museum (IWM), Imperial War Museum/E.T. Archive (IWM/ETA), *This England* (TE), Popperfoto (P), Robert Hunt (RH), Robert Harding Picture Library (RHPL)